"*Community* will inspire your small group leaders to grow and maintain healthy, Christ-centered, and mission-minded groups. It will be a vital tool for your pastors, church leaders, and small group leaders."

Craig Groeschel, Senior Pastor, LifeChurch.tv; author,
WEIRD: Because Normal Isn't Working

"Christianity is not for lone rangers. We are saved by Jesus to be a vital part of a team called the church—the body of Christ. *Community* is an excellent book that clearly, theologically, and practically helps us to see what it means to be a biblically functioning community on mission for Jesus. It answers the question 'Why have community groups?' and it provides a reproducible pattern as to how to implement them. Read it, then go and put its insights into practice."

Daniel L. Akin, President, Southeastern Baptist
Theological Seminary

"In the twentieth century, multitudes of churches grew through attractional evangelism and Sunday school classes on their property. In the twenty-first century, newer and growing churches focus missionally on community groups—not in educational buildings but in the homes of believers—scattered in the neighborhoods all around a church's region. This is a good thing. Pastor Brad House has written a fantastic book to help conventional, transitional, and emerging churches to live out the gospel in community. Read your Bible, then read this, and then go reach your neighbors."

Alvin L. Reid, Professor of Evangelism and Student Ministry,
Bailey Smith Chair of Evangelism, Southeastern Baptist
Theological Seminary

"I sincerely believe this book has the power to redefine small group ministry. With brilliance Brad unearths the theology behind micro-Christian communities, clarifies the role and realities of the gospel, and vividly describes the system, infrastructure, and strategy that Mars Hill has (through trial and error) found to be most effective. If your goal is to create gospel-centered small groups that make Jesus known on the streets, cul-de-sacs, and neighborhoods where God placed you to do ministry, read this book, reflect on what it says, and then make it your guide for doing groups."

Rick Howerton, author, *Destination Community: Small-Group Ministry Manual*

"In a rare combination, Brad House bridges the biblical and theological underpinnings of small groups and presents practical *how-tos*. He explains why smaller communities are imperative to the health of the individual and to the church, and then goes on to explain from bottom to top how to make it work in your church. Free of clichés and stereotypes, Brad takes a fresh look at an ancient concept!"

Bill Search, author, *Simple Small Groups*; Small Groups Pastor,
Southeast Christian Church

"When people think of Mars Hill Church in Seattle, they probably imagine a big church that's big on preaching. In this helpful book, Brad House shows that Mars Hill is far more than that. But this book isn't merely a description of how Mars Hill does small groups. This is a thoughtful and thorough treatment of the what, why, and even how of gospel-centered, community-focused, mission-shaped small groups. I've been doing church this way for years, and there is a great deal in here to help me as I learn how to do life-on-life together on mission with the people of God."

Steve Timmis, director, Acts 29 Western Europe;
coauthor *Total Church*

"Brad provides a compelling vision and clear strategy for incarnational, missional group life in churches. It is shaped by Scripture, forged in the crucible of trial and error, supported by a common-sense structure, and transferable to any church willing to do the gutsy work of community building in a world that desperately needs it."

Bill Donahue, founder, The Communitas Network; best-selling author,
Leading Life-Changing Small Groups

Community

COMMUNITY
TAKING YOUR SMALL GROUP OFF LIFE SUPPORT

BRAD HOUSE
FOREWORD BY MARK DRISCOLL

:: CROSSWAY

WHEATON, ILLINOIS

Cover design: Patrick Mahoney of The Mahoney Design Team

Cover image: Patrick Mahoney

First printing 2011

Printed in the United States of America

ISBN-13: 978-1-4335-2306-9
ISBN-10: 1-4335-2306-X
PDF ISBN: 978-1-4335-2315-1
Mobipocket ISBN: 978-1-4335-2316-8
EPub ISBN: 978-1-4335-2317-5

Library of Congress Cataloging-in-Publication Data
House, Brad, 1976–
    Community : taking your small group off life support / Brad House ; foreword by Mark Driscoll.
      p. cm.
    Includes bibliographical references.
    ISBN 978-1-4335-2306-9 (tp)
    1. Church group work. 2. Small groups—Religious aspects—Christianity. I. Title.
BV652.2.H68   2011
253'.7—dc22   2011014458

Crossway is a publishing ministry of Good News Publishers.

VP		20	19	18	17	16	15	14	13	12	11
14	13	12	11	10	9	8	7	6	5	4	3	2	1

To my gorgeous wife,
simply, thank you.

CONTENTS

FOREWORD

Most churches are considerably better at either the attractional ministry of gathering people to events and programs or the missional ministry of scattering people in groups and community. Jesus and the apostles did both in their ministries. By God's grace we can too. When we do, like using two pedals on a bike, the church moves forward quickly on mission in culture.

Since the launch of Mars Hill Church in the fall of 1996, we have been better at the attractional side of ministry (what we call the air war). People came to church on Sundays, heard the Word preached, repented of sin, trusted in Jesus, sang in worship, partook of Communion, and were baptized. However, we were very weak at the missional side of ministry (what we call the ground war), so that even when we were a church of thousands, we had only a handful of groups and no mechanism by which to mobilize people for mission in their neighborhoods. To be sure, many people self-organized informally and some ministry was done. But it was not as dynamic or effective as it could have been. We tried many times to get our small groups ministry to work, but with no success.

Everything changed once we added community groups who follow the preaching. Now we gather under the Word of God to then scatter for the mission of God. The results have been staggering. Our church has grown deeper in service, justice, love, unity, evangelism, care, and community as it has grown larger. Our pastors are spending more time than ever training people to do ministry, as our people are on mission leading hundreds and hundreds and hundreds of community groups.

So many people have inquired about community groups that we asked my friend and neighbor, Pastor Brad House, to write this book. I am grateful that he has, because I want your church to grow both bigger and deeper by the grace of God. The concepts he shares are not theory; they are reality. They are not summaries from the latest books on community and mission, but rather reports from the front lines of one of America's fastest-growing and largest churches in what used to be among the nation's least-churched cities. They are not faddish, but rather deeply rooted in the Bible and the best of two thousand years of faithful Christian ministry, which means they work across contexts. For example, at Mars Hill there are campuses with hundreds of people and campuses with thousands of people. There are campuses with a wide diversity of races, cultures, and ages, and campuses that are less diverse. Some campuses are composed of mainly single people whereas others have mainly married couples and families. We have services in our home city of Seattle and services outside the state of Washington entirely. Despite all these differences, there is one similarity—besides Jesus, of course—community groups are working and growing by God's grace. We hope and pray they would at your church, as well.

I would particularly encourage the primary preaching pastor at every church to read this book and champion the cause of community groups. From the pulpit you can lead the church on mission through the groups. The heart of this concept is to take what you do on Sundays and multiply it in the community, equipping your people for and sending them on mission to their neighborhoods together. You are vital to this cause. It cannot get or sustain momentum without you. Your people get excited about what you are excited about. So, please read this book and get excited about community groups!

Pastor Mark Driscoll

ACKNOWLEDGMENTS

I could not write a book on community without thanking the community that inspired, encouraged, and assisted me in the conception and development of this work.

First, I want to thank my wife, Jill, and our three awesome kids. I love you guys, and your support and encouragement soothed the challenges that came from writing and kept me smiling throughout the process.

Likewise, I want to thank the elders of Mars Hill Church for your support and the opportunity to follow the call that God has placed on my life. Thank you for your unapologetic passion for Jesus, your unwavering submission to God's Word, and your commitment to proclaiming the gospel. Specifically, I want to thank Mark Driscoll for encouraging me to write and for his leadership at Mars Hill.

A few men have been of personal encouragement to me as I was writing this book: Tim Beltz, Bill Clem, and Scott Thomas. Many others have encouraged me, but your words and confidence in me were instrumental.

Justin Holcomb, Matt Johnson, and Mike Wilkerson deserve appreciation for their theological review and comments that helped refine my thoughts and ideas.

That said, this book would have never seen the light of day without the army of God's ambassadors, the community group leaders and coaches of Mars Hill Church. Thank you for your sacrifices and your passion for the gospel. Without you this book is just ideas. You have made it a reality.

LIST OF CHARTS AND DIAGRAMS

DIAGNOSIS:
AN INTRODUCTION

CRITICAL CONDITION

Paul begins his first letter to the Corinthian church with these words:

> To the church of God that is in Corinth, to those sanctified in Christ Jesus, called to be saints together with all those who in every place call upon the name of our Lord Jesus Christ, both their Lord and ours: Grace to you and peace from God our Father and the Lord Jesus Christ. I give thanks to my God always for you because of the grace of God that was given you in Christ Jesus.[1]

These words are amazing because the bulk of the letter that follows is Paul rebuking and correcting these "saints" for their sin, lack of knowledge, and, ultimately, their poor witness of the gospel through which they were saved. In this letter we can see Paul's love and concern for the church, culminating in his charge to "be steadfast, immovable, always abounding in the work of the Lord."[2] He wants to see their lives transformed so that the work of the Lord can be accomplished. Paul is concerned with the legacy of the church in Corinth. He is not satisfied with them merely hearing or knowing the gospel. But it is not that Paul wants the church to *do more*. He wants them to *be more*. I am convinced that he is not disappointed with the church as much as he desires to see them live abundant lives that reflect what Jesus has already done.[3]

Fast-forward to the church today. What do you think Paul would write to us? Do you think if he sat in on a typical small group meeting he would be satisfied with the state of the church? Would he see us living as one body with each part working in harmony for the glory of God in all things?

Sadly, community within the church today is hemorrhaging. Giving in to the pressures of our culture to do more and fill every gap with entertainment has pushed community to the margins. We don't have time to invest in people and relationships. Our attention spans have dwindled to two-minute sound bites on YouTube. We can only invest 140 characters in our relationships.

The answer to such social fragmentation can be found in small groups. Yet small groups, at least in the traditional way we envision them, are not solidifying community as we thought. As we will discuss in chapter 2, one study indicates that less than 18 percent of young evangelicals ages eighteen to twenty-three participate in a small group, Bible study, or prayer group that is sponsored by their local churches. This disconnection is concerning. Paul tells us in 1 Corinthians 12 that we need every member of the body to participate in the life of the church, and when one member suffers the whole body suffers. If that is the case, what happens when 82 percent of the body is completely missing?

Several years ago, a longtime leader came up to me one day and told me that he was done. He just couldn't lead a group any longer. He said that it was draining him of energy and time and, in his words, "sucking the life out of [him]." Surprised, I asked him why it was so draining. He proceeded to describe a typical small group meeting: three hours, lots of preparations for hosting and the Bible study, awkward circles—you know the drill. I asked him what it would look like for that group to be life giving, and he painted a gripping picture of a Christ-centered community. When I asked him why he didn't lead his group to that picture, he replied that he didn't know he could.

If we are going to take our groups off life support, we are going to need permission to reimagine what gospel-centered community looks like. We will not change the preconceived view of groups by making participation a requirement for membership or by changing the names of our programs from "ministries" to "groups." Small groups will thrive when they become the place where we experience life-giving transformation.

I, like Paul and many others, am concerned with the legacy of the church. That is why I wrote this book. The number of seats we fill will not determine the legacy of our churches. The depth to which the gospel penetrates those lives will determine our legacy. I have no qualms about large churches so long as they are committed to seeing the gospel transform the people in them. I want to see as many lives as possible saved and transformed by Jesus. My heart and conviction is that we can, and will, see lives transformed through authentic, gospel-centered community that is inspired by the power and wonder of God.

We cannot be content with the status quo of today's church. Foundational to this work is the conviction that we were created for more, we have been redeemed for more, and we are empowered for more. This does not mean that we need to do more, but that we *are* more through the reconciling work of Jesus.

In this book, I join the chorus of leaders calling the sleeping church to wake up and "abound in the work of the Lord" because his grace has made it possible. I endeavor to affirm community as a gift of God's grace for the purpose of exalting the Son and making him known. In other words, community is not about us; it is about God. Community is an instrument of worship, a weapon against sin, and a tool for evangelism—all for the exaltation of Jesus.

A lot must change for this to become reality. In his book *Don't Waste Your Life* and his sermon series on the book of Romans, John Piper calls for having a wartime mentality when it comes to the Christian life.[4] We are fighting for the glory of God and the souls of our neighbors, who are casualties in the fray. To paraphrase *Don't Waste Your Life*, the church has been lulled into believing that we are in a time of peace. We often live lives of comfort, nonchalantly going about our business as if we are safe from the dangers of war. Yet Scripture tells us that Satan prowls around like a lion waiting to devour us.[5] Peter declares that sin is waging war against our souls.[6] Paul encourages us to fight the good fight and hold firmly to the faith as if someone were trying to rip it from us.[7] This does not sound like peace. These verses and many others are brilliantly prophetic of the reality in which we live. Every day we see the casualties of this war. That is, if our eyes are open. The effects of sin are ravaging our friends and neighbors, not to mention the church itself. The question is, Are we going to fight?

As I survey the landscape of the church today, especially as I get behind the curtain and look at how people actually live their lives, I see a church that has little signs of life. We appear to be breathing as we gather for worship services and run our programs, but oftentimes we are merely surviving rather than living life abundantly. Jesus tells us that we must lose our lives if we want to save them. Life should be defined as the passionate pursuit of God. It should be marked by a hatred of sin in the believer's life and an unquenchable desire for the fame of Jesus, taking every opportunity to share the gospel with a fallen world. If that is life, how are your vital signs? Can you find a pulse in the community of your church?

We have tried everything to prop up community within the church in hopes that it will spring back to life. We inject it with mission statements as if a shot of adrenaline will get things started. This leads to short bursts of excitement that fade just as quickly. We build programs to relieve the pressure and weight of being in community, hoping that if we can breathe for our people, then they will be more apt to participate. Unfortunately, the opposite happens, and they become dependent on feeding tubes and iron lungs.

In the end we may be able to sustain a pulse, but it is hard to call it life. It is artificial and plastic. People gather in small groups for discussions, but lives are not transformed by the gospel. Real life begets more life. It changes lives and transforms cities. I want us to have that kind of life. That is the life that is promised through Christ. That is the life that we receive from God. When Jesus said that he came that we might live life abundantly, this is what he was talking about—life that is empowered by the Spirit, exalts the Son, and glorifies the Father.

Artificial life is static, tethered to a system or program that sustains it. I want our churches to experience life off of the machines, life that is actively responding to the grace that has been poured out on us. It is my prayer that the ideas in this book will help you to breathe life back into community in a way that will not only rally the church to action, but also give your people a means of building a strategy to advance the kingdom in the context of where they live.

DEFINING TERMS

COMMUNITY GROUP

You will hear this term frequently. *Community group* refers to the scattered church grouping that may be known more commonly by the moniker *small group*. You may call yours care groups, missional communities, life groups, or fried chicken. The point is that we are generally talking about the same small unit of community within the greater body of the church. Now, although I suggest that the name is not the point, I should mention that nomenclature is significant. The name you choose could have an inspirational or limiting effect on the expression of that community. Care groups, for example, have a hard time engaging missionally in culture because when a person joins a care group, he or she expects to be cared for, not to be challenged to evangelize. On the other hand, missional communities will theoretically have the opposite dilemma. With that said, *community groups* is not the perfect name or the only name for such communities, but it has served us well at Mars Hill Church, and I will use it in the remainder of this book.

CHURCH

I will borrow the definition of *church* from Mark Driscoll and Gerry Breshears in *Vintage Church*:

> The local church is a community of regenerated believers who confess Jesus Christ as Lord. In obedience to Scripture they organize under qualified leadership, gather regularly for preaching and worship, observe the biblical sacraments of baptism and

Communion, are unified by the Spirit, are disciplined for holiness, and scatter to fulfill the Great Commandment and the Great Commission as missionaries to the world for God's glory and their joy.[8]

Important in this definition is the truth that the church is a community of God's people gathered for his mission. Therefore, when I speak of the church in the following chapters, I am referring to the body of Christ, not an organization, the leadership apart from the body, or an abstraction. We are talking about flesh and blood, you and me.

MISSION
Buzzword of buzzwords in the church today, *mission* is still too valuable a concept to abandon. I will, however, take the time to define a broad definition of it. Although there may be specific nuances of the mission to which God has called your church, it must include the making and maturing of disciples. That is to say that the mission is to glorify God by proclaiming the gospel of Jesus for the sake of gathering God's people to him, and to teach and grow them in their knowledge and love of Christ. Jesus put it this way, "Go therefore and make disciples of all nations, baptizing them in the name of the Father and of the Son and of the Holy Spirit, teaching them to observe all that I have commanded you."[9] Therefore, when I speak of owning or living out the mission, it should be understood in these terms.

HEALTH PLAN
It has become cliché for a book on community groups to state that it is not advocating a program, but I will say it anyway. I am not advocating a new program. What this book is about is shaking the Etch A Sketch of what community groups are and how they function in the church. It seeks to expand the idea of what community groups could accomplish for the kingdom of God. In doing this, I want to bring together theology and ministry philosophy with practical application and strategy that is worked out with effectiveness. To accomplish this, the book is separated into three sections.

THE FOUNDATION: BUILDING BLOCKS FOR LIFE

Life in our community groups starts with building on the right foundation. The first section seeks to define these foundational principles of community. Starting with a theological background of what community is and God's purpose through it, we will address the motivation behind having community groups in your church and why they are essential. This section will address the purpose and need for community groups within the church and how they work together with other functions of the church, such as preaching and worship, to produce transformation in the lives of disciples. This section will also address the general state of our churches with regard to community and ownership within the body that is hamstringing the local church. We have been remiss, as the church, in creating systems and small group programs without anchoring them to the purposes revealed in Scripture. The purpose of this section is to challenge you to know why you are building a small group ministry before you ask the question of how.

HEALTH PLAN: REDEFINING COMMUNITY GROUPS

The second section applies the foundational principles from the first section to redefine what community is and how we employ it as a church. If we are going to rethink community, there is a great deal to blow up when it comes to the practical experience. Ironically, for "a holy nation, a people," we are comically pathetic at community.[10] Sadder still is the fact that the church's offering of "real community," which the world so desperately needs, is woefully short of the sales pitch. This section will address common pitfalls in the way we experience community that render it ineffective and obligatory rather than life giving. We will address strategic ways to organize and lead the church that encourage ownership, participation, and creativity. This section will also challenge us to think differently about community groups, including their function, rhythms, and engagement with culture. We will discuss ways in which your community groups can participate in the mission and work that God has ordained for your church.

TREATMENT: EFFECTING CHANGE IN YOUR GROUPS

Ever read the "how to draw" comic in the Sunday paper? In the first section you draw a circle. In the second section you draw two squares. Then in the last section you have a full-color drawing of the Mona Lisa. That is just plain mean. And it would be mean, or at least unfruitful, to paint a picture of a new way to experience community and not give you help in getting there. The last section will address how you get from where you are today to where you want to be in the future. We will take the time to address how change can occur on a large or small scale and give some practical examples of how you can inspire your church toward a new paradigm for community. This is not a plug-and-play way of living in community. It will require repentance, prayer, commitment, and patience. The result of living life in a way that glorifies Christ and encourages one another toward righteousness, though, will be worth it.

REDEFINED BY THE CROSS

Peter describes the church in this way:

> You are a chosen race, a royal priesthood, a holy nation, a people for his own possession, that you may proclaim the excellencies of him who called you out of darkness into his marvelous light. Once you were not a people, but now you are God's people; once you had not received mercy, but now you have received mercy.
>
> Beloved, I urge you as sojourners and exiles to abstain from the passions of the flesh, which wage war against your soul. Keep your conduct among the Gentiles honorable, so that when they speak against you as evildoers, they may see your good deeds and glorify God on the day of visitation.[11]

I want this for the church. This is who we are in Christ because of what Jesus has accomplished on the cross and through his resurrection. I want us to be a people who proclaim the excellencies of Jesus and whose conduct, through the transformation of the gospel, brings people to the cross. Imagine the effect that this would have on your city or town.

My good friend, Pastor Bill Clem, was preaching on community and summed up the conviction and passion I have for it. I was disappointed that he had coined the statement instead of me, but because we are in community, I like to think we said it. It went like this: "The world will not recover from the community of God's people living lives to glorify Jesus."[12] This statement should change the way you look at community in your church. We have the means to proclaim the kingdom of God through the same means God has always used: his people. The question is, Are we willing to count the cost, repent, and receive the blessing of community?

I love Jesus and I love his church. My prayer is that this book will be a blessing to you and your church as you rethink what it means to live in community for the glory of God. I pray that community groups would be a source of soul-satisfying life in your church. I pray that the name of Jesus will be exalted in your city through the witness of the body of Christ. I pray your city would never recover.

PART ONE

THE FOUNDATION: BUILDING BLOCKS FOR LIFE

BUILDING THE FOUNDATION

The purpose of this section is to lay a foundation for building a life-giving and life-sustaining community within your church. Illustrating the need for a solid foundation, Jesus said,

> Everyone then who hears these words of mine and does them will be like a wise man who built his house on the rock. And the rain fell, and the floods came, and the winds blew and beat on that house, but it did not fall, because it had been founded on the rock. And everyone who hears these words of mine and does not do them will be like a foolish man who built his house on the sand. And the rain fell, and the floods came, and the winds blew and beat against that house, and it fell, and great was the fall of it.[1]

I want us to be a church that has the confidence of a house built on the rock. Jesus calls us to dig deep into his Word and lay a solid foundation of faithfulness. We are called to hear his words, be changed by them, and to live out of the convictions brought by the Holy Spirit. He is telling us to build our lives on the foundation of faith and obedience in him, through the living Word of Scripture.

What an excellent foundation! Yet there are so many who build their foundations on sand rather than rock. When it comes to ministry, and community group ministries in particular, I see sloppy foundations. We can get so excited about a new innovative idea or opportunity to contextualize that we often skip this important step: build your foundation on the rock. Wind, rain, and floods will come in the form of sin, suffering, and tragedy. The question is, Will your community have the conviction to be the church when the flood comes, when Jake confesses to an addiction to porn, when Jane loses hope, when Tom loses his job?

A colleague relayed this story to me. An army friend of his was watching new recruits train on the shooting range when he noticed one young man standing at attention at the end of the range. He didn't know why the soldier was there, but now that he thought about it, there was always a soldier at attention at the end of the shooting range. He approached the officer in charge and asked why. The answer was, "That is how we have always done it." It was the protocol for firing on the range. Curious, his friend researched further. His findings were amusing. The protocol was written when officers rode horses. The young man at the end of the range was there to hold the horses' bridles so they would not get spooked from the gunshots. Though the officers no longer rode horses, the protocol was never changed, thus the lone soldier simply standing at attention at the end of the range.

It seems silly, but how many of us have never even asked why we have community groups at our churches? Having small groups at your church because of tradition or because that is what "successful" churches do is not a particularly sturdy foundation. It is like having no foundation at all and makes it fairly difficult to inspire a commitment to community.

So, before you begin building (or remodeling), let me encourage you with this: be like the wise man. Ask why before you ask how. Build your foundation before you pick out the drapes. We are so often in a hurry to fix the lack of authentic community within the church that we start building without a foundation. Jesus tells us not to be fools who put all our effort into building a house, picking out just the right hardwoods to accent the light in the family room, when it will all be washed away in the first storm. The goal of this section, and chapter 1 in particular, is to clearly define the foundation upon which we want to build our community groups so that they will stand up to the many storms that will come blowing through.

1

IMAGE

THE GOAL

Let me begin by acknowledging that building gospel-saturated community is not an easy task. Cain made it clear that the effects of the fall would throw a wrench in community and relationships in general. Starting with a poor biblical foundation increases that labor significantly. Lifeless community begins when we don't have a clear understanding of why we are in community in the first place. Yet, when we try to rejuvenate small groups, we generally ask how we can get more people in them, rather than addressing the question of why they exist. It is no surprise that we have a hard time attracting people to such a ministry.

Our goal here is bigger than increasing the number of groups we have in our churches. We want to reestablish the basis for community and why it is, and always has been, essential to the Christian life. Because community takes sacrifice and intentionality, our view of community must be bigger than a way to belong, making church feel smaller, or closing the back door of the church. We need to see the eternal purpose in order to inspire the devotion to community that we see in Acts 2.

A GOOD THING BROKEN

You see, the problem is deeper than the need to belong. On the cross, the community of the Trinity was momentarily broken.[1] It was a picture of what sin always does to communities. Sin always separates what God joins together. This truth is seen in Adam's response to the fall. The first thing that Adam and Eve did in response to their rebellion was hide from God.[2] God intended for Adam and Eve to be fruitful and multiply, thereby building communities that would glorify him. Instead, because of indwelling sin, each community was more rebellious than the last, manifesting in relational evil against one another. That moment on the cross was a reflection of our sins of independence, selfishness, rivalry, jealousy, oppression, blame shifting, gossip, backbiting, neglect, isolation, pride, apathy, and every other perversion of grace that destroys community.

There are a couple of problems with a life that perverts grace in this way. First, it is a distorted picture of what God himself is like. A community of God's people should reflect the nature of God. A community that is marked more by sin than by grace and claims to be a community formed by God misrepresents the Creator. Second, it denies grace by choosing an impoverished and deprived life. The community God creates is good because it reflects him; it is good for his people. Choosing a life outside of community with God denies this truth and is what got us in this mess in the first place.

Christians certainly aren't the only ones to lament the fragmentation of society. Christian or not, we all have an intrinsic need for community. We all suffer from the isolation that sin breeds. Our neighbors are desperate to belong and be connected to a people. Some try to rebuild community through social action, campaigns, planning better cities, revitalizing neighborhood schools, or feeding the homeless. Others join gangs or social clubs, immerse themselves in virtual communities online, or hang out in coffee shops. These are all attempts to satisfy the need for community, but the problem is, none of these solutions address the real problem. They don't address the cause of isolation.

The sin that disintegrates our communities and alienates us from one another is what put Jesus on the cross. He experienced the worst isolation and the worst evil—separation from God the Father. He was relationally severed from the eternal community of the

Trinity. In trade, he gave us the greatest good, reconciliation to God and others, making community possible.

REBUILT ON THE CROSS

But let's be honest, we have all fallen short of community that proclaims the truth of God's goodness and grace, as we are often censored by fear or muzzled by sin. The cross, then, is central to building community within the church. If the church is going to offer an alternative to the brokenness and isolation in the world, then it must be a community that is transformed by the death and resurrection of Jesus.

In Ephesians 2:15b–22, we see the intentionality behind the cross in building (or rebuilding) the community of God:

> That he might create in himself one new man in place of the two, so making peace, and might *reconcile us both to God in one body through the cross*, thereby killing the hostility. And he came and preached peace to you who were far off and peace to those who were near. For through him we both have access in one Spirit to the Father. So then *you are no longer strangers and aliens*, but you are fellow citizens with the saints and members of the household of God, *built on the foundation of the apostles and prophets, Christ Jesus himself being the cornerstone*, in whom the whole structure, being joined together, grows into a holy temple in the Lord. In him you also are being built together into a dwelling place for God by the Spirit.

In this text we see that we are a community of believers built on the cornerstone of Jesus. This work is completed and we need only to receive it. Through Christ we are fellow citizens and members of one household reconciled through the cross. We are saved to be a community, not a church of individuals. Dietrich Bonhoeffer sums it up this way: "Christian community means community through and in Jesus Christ."[3] It is through Christ that we have been reconciled to God and to one another. It is in Christ that we are united together like a family who shares the bloodline of Jesus. Jesus gives us the ability to experience life as God intended, in real community with him and one another. In a world searching for belonging, the cross is a beacon of hope. We belong to one another because we have been united in Christ.

The purpose of such community is to display the love of God for the world. We see this design just a few verses earlier in Ephesians 2 when Paul explains why we have been made alive in Christ. He says that it was "so that in the coming ages he might show the immeasurable riches of his grace in kindness toward us in Christ Jesus."[4] This is the purpose of community. We have been saved so that we would express the gospel of Jesus Christ. Living together in community, reconciled and united by the cross, is a physical demonstration of the grace of God.

Community is for us a declaration of the overwhelming love of God, a tangible proclamation of the reconciling work of the cross. This is a truly compelling reason to build community groups within our churches. This is the bigger purpose that can inspire real community. Community groups are a living illustration of the gospel and its power to save. The world needs this, and so does your church.

CREATED FOR COMMUNITY

Understanding why community is essential to the life of the Christian and the proclamation of the gospel begins with understanding that we were created for community.

No one really debates the need for people to exist within community. It is not merely a Christian understanding; it is a human understanding. But belonging in and of itself will never be enough. Hanging the need for community on belonging is like hanging the need for water on thirst. The need for both is deeper. Thirst is a symptom of a deeper design—that your body was created to require water to survive. While we can technically survive without community, we don't function properly without it. The deeper need for community is embedded in the very fabric of who we are; it is part of our design.

Ask people who they are and you will get plenty of different answers. We often define ourselves by what we do or what we have. This identity determines how we see ourselves and affects every choice we make. Distortions in our identity lead us to search for fulfillment in places other than God and to settle for less than what God intended. If our identity is wrapped up in being self-sufficient and autonomous, then we will likely never experience life-giving community. Start in the wrong place and it really doesn't matter how good the map is.

Because Jesus has redeemed us, we can reset our identity to reside in the place God intended. When Jesus reconciled us to the Father, he established for us a renewed identity. This identity is a restoration of the image of God in which we were created.

In Genesis, at the pinnacle of creation, God creates mankind. The Bible records that God said, "Let us make man in our image, after our likeness."[5] When God says he is going to make man in his image, he informs us of our intended identity. We are image bearers of God. We exist as a living reflection of God, who exists in eternal community.[6]

In other words, God exists in an eternal relationship within the Godhead of Father, Son, and Holy Spirit. As a relational being, he creates us as relational beings to represent him to all of creation. God solidifies this point in the creation story of man in Genesis 2. He makes a point of expressing the incompleteness of man apart from community when he says, "It is not good that the man should be alone."[7] Scripture emphasizes that we cannot image God's relational nature in isolation.

So what does this mean? This means that we were created for community. We were not created simply to appreciate it. We are incomplete without it.

Furthermore, by God's grace, through the death and resurrection of Jesus, he made true community possible. Jesus restored the image of God that was marred by sin. Jesus made it possible for us to reflect the relational nature of God through life in community. When we live in community as a declaration of the gospel, we announce that Jesus has restored what sin had broken, and we experience life as God intended.

CREATED TO GLORIFY GOD

We have established that indeed we were created for community, but why? Being an image bearer is not only a description of who we are;

it is also a description of why we are. We are created as a reflection of God (who we are) to reflect God to all of creation (why we are). The eternal purpose of mankind is to proclaim the glory of God to the world. The Westminster Shorter Catechism says as much when it declares that "Man's chief end is to glorify God, and to enjoy him forever."[8] We do this as we receive, believe, and celebrate what has been done through the death and resurrection of Jesus.

Reflecting the glory of God as an image bearer is to proclaim who God is through our lives. God reveals his nature to us in this way:

> The LORD, the LORD, a God merciful and gracious, slow to anger, and abounding in steadfast love and faithfulness, keeping steadfast love for thousands, forgiving iniquity and transgression and sin, but who will by no means clear the guilty, visiting the iniquity of the fathers on the children and the children's children, to the third and the fourth generation.[9]

This is the nature of God that we are to reflect in Christ-centered community. A community of God should be merciful, gracious, slow to anger, and abounding in steadfast love and faithfulness. They are a people who address sin with compassion and patience and are quick to restore the repentant. Paul puts it this way in his letter to the Colossians:

> Put on then, as God's chosen ones, holy and beloved, compassionate hearts, kindness, humility, meekness, and patience, bearing with one another and, if one has a complaint against another, forgiving each other; as the Lord has forgiven you, so you also must forgive. And above all these put on love, which binds everything together in perfect harmony. And let the peace of Christ rule in your hearts, to which indeed you were called in one body. And be thankful. Let the word of Christ dwell in you richly, teaching and admonishing one another in all wisdom, singing psalms and hymns and spiritual songs, with thankfulness in your hearts to God. And whatever you do, in word or deed, do everything in the name of the Lord Jesus, giving thanks to God the Father through him.[10]

This is a picture of a community reflecting the attributes of God because of what Jesus has done. Christ-centered community allows us to reflect the relational nature of God as well as his mercy and grace. It is a community that confronts sin and forgives one another, marked by compassion, kindness, humility, meekness, and patience. It is a community that seeks to live in peace with one another and reconcile broken relationships. That is dramatically different than the way the world handles conflict. When Christ reconciled us to one another on the cross, he made such a reflection possible.

Reflecting the image of God was a gift to mankind that was not shared with any other created being. Yet it is a gift that we forfeited through sin and rebellion. Jesus purchased and restores this precious gift through the cross. And when we then exalt Jesus, we glorify the Father and fulfill our call as image bearers to proclaim the greatness of God.

It is not enough to say that we should live out our faith in community because we are image bearers of the Trinitarian God. We are image bearers of a Trinitarian God who have been redeemed by the death, burial, and resurrection of Jesus. Our lives in community are a proclamation of who God is and what God has done through our Savior.

INSPIRED BY HIS GLORY

This understanding inspires a life and community devoted to Jesus. The motivation that will sustain such community is not the expectation to glorify God; it is the glory of God itself. In other words, you can't just tell people that they *should* glorify God. We need to see the beauty, the splendor, and the magnificence of our God. A clear view of God puts life in perspective. It is simultaneously terrifying and motivating. When we see God clearly, we understand that there is nothing more important than worshiping him and lifting up his name.

Isaiah saw the glory of God in the temple and he was a mess.[11] He was so aware of his sin and the sin of his people that he thought he would die in the midst of God. That experience changed Isaiah and the way he lived his life. After seeing God's majesty, he was willing to do anything to proclaim the majesty of the Father. When asked who would go to proclaim the truth of God, Isaiah volunteered without hesitation. He did not ask what he was being sent to do. He did not ask what he would receive in return. He just went.

We see the same pattern in Moses, David, Peter, and Paul. These men were all inspired by the glory of God to live lives that reflected his splendor. Peter is my favorite of the bunch. Prone to write checks with his mouth that his body could not cash, something changed in Peter after he witnessed the resurrection of Jesus. Before the resurrection, Peter boasted of going to his death for Jesus but was so intimidated by the questions of a teenage girl that he denied Christ altogether.[12] However, after witnessing the splendor of God through the resurrected Jesus, Peter preached with boldness until he was crucified upside down for his faith.[13]

So why are our communities so apathetic and paralyzed by fear of man? We, too, have seen the glory of God. The Gospel of John tells us that "the Word became flesh and dwelt among us, and we have seen his glory, glory as of the only Son from the Father, full of grace and truth. (John bore witness about him, and cried out, 'This was he of whom I said, "He who comes after me ranks before me, because he was before me.")') And from his fullness we have all received, grace upon grace."[14] Not only have we seen him, but also we have received his grace. How much more should we be inspired to live in a community that exalts the Son?

Through his letter to Timothy, Paul tells us to "Remember Jesus Christ, risen from the dead, the offspring of David, as preached in my gospel, for which I am suffering, bound with chains as a criminal. But the word of God is not bound! Therefore I endure everything for the sake of the elect, that they also may obtain the salvation that is in Christ Jesus with eternal glory."[15] Now that is a man who has seen the goodness of God and knows that Jesus is worthy to be worshiped. The death and resurrection of Christ inspired Paul to live a life submitted to the will of the Father. The grace of God displayed through the Son sustained Paul through suffering and pain. He was willing to "endure everything" for the chance to be a part of God's saving work in the world.

That is the kind of community we want to build. We want a people who have such a clear view of Jesus that temporal circumstances do not make them waiver from their call to make disciples. If we are going to call the church to live out the gospel through the storms of life, we need this kind of inspiration.

EMPOWERED BY HIS GRACE

While God's glory inspires obedience, it is empowered by his grace. Isaiah was right to be afraid to be in the presence of God. But God in his grace cleansed him of his sin so that he could respond to God's call. God not only inspires us through his glory, he also gives us the ability to respond through his grace. This is the beauty of the atoning work of Jesus on the cross. We have been reconciled so that we can image him to the world, and he sends us the Holy Spirit to empower us to such a life.[16] Second Peter says, "His divine power has given us everything we need for a godly life through our knowledge of him who called us by his own glory and goodness."[17] This is God's promise for transformational community.

So what does a community inspired by the glory of God and empowered by grace look like? As we receive his grace we are able to be a reflection of his goodness. A community that has been transformed by the gospel reflects the nature of God. One of my favorite pictures of who we are to be as a community can be found in 1 Peter 2:9–12:

> But you are a chosen race, a royal priesthood, a holy nation, a people for his own possession, that you may proclaim the excellencies of him who called you out of darkness into his marvelous light. Once you were not a people, but now you are God's people; once you had not received mercy, but now you have received mercy.
>
> Beloved, I urge you as sojourners and exiles to abstain from the passions of the flesh, which wage war against your soul. Keep your conduct among the Gentiles honorable, so that when they speak against you as evildoers, they may see your good deeds and glorify God on the day of visitation.

What a great description of community. The context here is that we are being built up as a spiritual house of God, just as Paul declared in Ephesians 2.[18] This then is a picture of the church. It is a community of people transformed by the gospel.

Peter begins with reminding us of our identity. We are "a chosen race, a royal priesthood, a holy nation, a people for his own possession."[19] We have a new identity that comes from our faith in Christ and binds us together. Christ has purchased this identity, so we are *already* "a chosen race, a royal priesthood, a holy nation, a people for his own possession."[20] We simply need to *be* what Jesus has already secured for us in his death and resurrection. Notice then, that this identity is corporate rather than individual. While my personal identity is in Jesus, Peter makes it clear that we have a communal identity, as well.

Christianity is not an individual sport. We are part of a team. For our community groups to mature and image God, we need to see ourselves as a people connected by Jesus. We have to be more than a collection of individuals who occasionally gather together. We need a corporate sense of our identity. A gospel-centered community will find their identity in Jesus individually and corporately.

Peter then gives us the reason for which God made us a community. He says it is "*that you may* proclaim the excellencies" of the one who saved us.[21] This is more than a description of a Christian community. This is the purpose of community. We are to worship Jesus as a people and declare the good news that a Savior has come. The natural expression of gratitude for a community that has been reconciled from death to life will be marked by worship and proclamation. We do this through remembering what he has done for us, calling us out of the isolation caused by sin and back into relationship with the Father.[22]

Next we see sanctification as an outworking of the gospel in community.[23] We are to be sanctified by living lives together that are honoring to God and marked by growth and maturation. Bonhoeffer anchors the goal of Christian community in "meet[ing] one another as bringers of the message of salvation."[24] That is because it is through the gospel that we are continuously being sanctified. A life-giving community is one that is continuously being transformed by the gospel as a people.

To illustrate this point, Peter says that we are in a "war" for our souls.[25] In boxing, you fight alone; in war, you fight as a nation. Sanctification is not an individual fight; it is one we fight as a community. By speaking the gospel to one another and living out its implications, we participate in a corporate sanctification process. This is true community.

Finally, Peter tells us to protect our witness among our neighbors.[26] He expects such a community to be seen by those who have yet to meet Jesus. There is an assumption that the way we live together is seen and points to Christ. Honorable conduct, or holiness, is not required to earn our righteousness; instead, it is an outworking of the gospel work in us that testifies to the power of the cross.[27]

Jesus makes this point to his disciples during the Last Supper when he tells them, "A new commandment I give to you, that you love one another: just as I have loved you, you also are to love one another. By this all people will know that you are my disciples, if you have love for one another."[28] Thus, he calls us to love one another in ways that can be seen by all men so that they know we live this way because of Jesus. Our primary purpose in community is not that our needs are being met, but that Jesus would be lifted up. It is not that we aren't blessed by the love we share for one another, but that we experience our greatest joy when Jesus is most glorified.[29]

Basically, the witness of community is more powerful than an individual witness. Loving your neighbors is much easier if you never have to deal with them. Living in light of the gospel is much harder in community where people sin against you. Your neighbors know this and that is why talk is cheap. Experiencing a people who confess their sins against one another, repent, and forgive is foreign to the world. Communities that live in this way, transformed by the gospel, will not only have a good reputation among their neighbors, but also they will point them to hope in Jesus. This is a community that has joined the mission of God.

And what is the ultimate goal of our neighbors seeing how we live? It is so they will worship God![30] Having our identity in Jesus— out of which flows worship of God, community with one another, and mission to the world—culminates in God being worshiped on the last day. Indeed, in this passage "Peter sees the priestly nature of the church as 'declaring the praises' of our exodus God and living in such a way among the nations that they come to glorify God."[31] The functions of community build toward this goal as we are empowered by his grace to live out gospel-centered community.

COMMUNITY IS NOT OPTIONAL

Community groups are essential to the Christian life because we were created for community. We were built to function in relationship with one another and with God. We are able to do so through the grace and reconciliation made possible by the death and resurrection of Jesus. Community, therefore, is an expression of who God is in Trinitarian relationship and a testimony to his love in redeeming us as a people through Jesus.

We must conclude that if God created community for this purpose, it should be an essential part of every Christian's life. The marginalization of community within the church and culture has not come from conviction but from apathy and isolation brought on by sin. Isolation is our response to sin. Community is our response to reconciliation.[32]

When we don't ask why we have community, it becomes a secondary function of the church rather than the primary vehicle through which God moves and makes his glory known. To resuscitate life in the community of God, we must reestablish the foundational purpose of community. We must root it in the cross.

If we want to take our small group communities off life support, we need to go to the source. We need the atoning work of Jesus that brings the dead to life. It is the gospel that plucked us from death, and it is the gospel that will breathe life into our anemic communities.

The inspiration for community is the death and resurrection of Jesus. It is the glimpse of his glorious return. It is the power over sin. It is his victory over death. As we receive the gift of grace and believe in the promise of what Jesus accomplished, we are compelled by the grace of our Savior to proclaim this great act of love. Living grace-filled lives in a community marked by humility and love, which seeks to reconcile one to another and broken lives to God, is the perfect means for such a proclamation.

We do not have community groups to close the back door of the church. We do not have groups because people need to belong or we need to care for one another. These are good but secondary effects of authentic community. These effects are not the foundation. We have community groups because we have seen the glory of God[33] and we have been given the grace to live our lives to exalt the Christ.[34] We have community groups because we have been reconciled to God and one another. We once were not a people but now we are a people of God's own possession.[35] We have community groups as a proclamation of the goodness of our God and testimony to the completed work of the cross. This is the foundation for gospel-saturated community that will overflow with life.

Call your people to meditate on the purpose of community. Seeing the eternal purpose purchased by the blood of Jesus will inspire the kind of devotion we see in the Acts 2 and 1 Peter 2 churches and that we desperately want to see lived out in the body of Christ.

2

BODY

DEFINING THE CENTER

In their book *Total Church*, Steve Timmis and Tim Chester begin their discussion on the importance of community as a central principle for how we do church with this quote by Sinclair Ferguson:

> The church lies at the very center of the eternal purpose of God. It is not a divine afterthought. It is not an accident of history. On the contrary, the church is God's new community. For His purpose, conceived in a past eternity, being worked out in history, and to be perfected in a future eternity, is not just to save isolated individuals and so perpetuate our loneliness but rather to build His church, that is, to call out of the world a people for His own glory.[1]

They argue convincingly and biblically that community is central to our identity as Christians and crucial for the mission of the church. As we established in the previous chapter, community is a gift of God's grace and essential for the Christian life. As Timmis, Chester, and Ferguson have suggested, this idea should transform our lives and inform the way we function as a body. Community is not a peripheral ministry. *Our communities should be the most palpable expression of the gospel within the church.*

As culture reflects the values of its citizens, community groups reflect the values of the church. If our church does not place a high value on community, then we are already disconnected from the convictions we discussed in the previous chapter. My experience has been that most churches consider community a value, but many have a hard time living out that value in a way that is visible and recognizable.

The church is constantly pulled to do so many things that it can be easy to neglect or devalue community groups within the sea of programs the church provides. If, however, we are going to breathe life back into the community of the church and see it function as God designed, we need to start thinking differently. Social justice, overseas missions, youth programs, food banks, sports ministries, and so on are acceptable programs, but they are not the center of God's mission, as Ferguson points out. They are support tools through which a gospel-saturated community can intentionally engage the world.

If we put all our energies into the tangential and neglect the center, we have no fertile ground where people can land and grow. I have heard such tangential ministries described as a funnel, drawing people into the church as they swirl toward the center. Ignoring the visual similarity to being flushed, the problem with a funnel is that it has a hole in the center. Fittingly, this has also been my experience when we neglect building the body of Christ. In order to breathe life back into your small group ministry, you must have a clear sense of its value and importance to your church. You cannot hope to gain momentum and life in such a ministry while simultaneously marginalizing it through resource allocation or ministry dilution. Elevating community groups to the proper (and balanced) level of significance is critical for breathing life back into your small group ministry.

IMPLICATIONS

If then we agree that community is essential for disciples of Jesus and that it is at the center of God's purpose, then we must expect implications for the church in form and function. If community is vital, then it should have a prominent role in the life of the church. Making community groups a primary ministry within the church elevates them above the peripheral ministries and will be key to creating momentum.

Unfortunately, though, I am not sure the church at large knows what to do with community groups. Most have some conviction that they are necessary but relegate them to a form of social day care. We have been content with *having* community groups rather than *employing* them to advance the kingdom of God. It is no wonder that many in the church today find community groups obligatory and a waste of energy.

I have recently noticed a trend of churches giving up on the notion that community is an essential component of church life. Many are deciding that community is an optional experience that is helpful but not elemental to being a healthy disciple of Jesus. I think this is a significant mistake. There is no biblical support for personal, autonomous Christianity. If we want to truly make disciples that advance the gospel, we must not only see the importance of community, we must understand it to be essential to the church.

So how are we, the church, doing at championing community as a primary ministry within the church? The National Study of Youth and Religion (2008)[2] reports that among young adults in the United States ages eighteen to twenty-three years, 15.2 percent of them say that they are currently involved in any organized religious group, such as Bible study, prayer group, or other religious group, not including regular worship service attendance. Among this group of young adults who identify as evangelical Christian, this number increases to 25 percent. Let me reiterate this point: *Nationwide, only one-quarter of young persons, eighteen to twenty-three years of age, who identify as evangelical Christian and/or attend an evangelical church[3] are currently involved in a community group or Bible study.*

Furthermore, among those evangelical Christians who are currently involved in a community group and currently attend religious services at a church, more than one-third (36.6 percent) report that the religious small group in which they participate is not a part of that church. Calculating this all out, this equates to the fact that among young evangelical Christians[4] ages eighteen to twenty-three in the United States today, only 17.3 percent of them are currently participating in an evangelical Christian community group or Bible study that is hosted by a church they attend. And among all emerging adults ages eighteen to twenty-three in the United States today, only 5.8 percent are currently participating in an evangelical Christian community group or Bible study that is hosted by a church they attend. This is debilitating to the church and reflects the true value that we place on living out our faith in community. Neglect breeds apathy and leads to death for a small group ministry. Life can only be regained when we reestablish the appropriate value within the church.

FUNCTIONS OF THE CHURCH

This we do know: God uses his people to accomplish his purposes. From the garden to Noah to Israel to the disciples, God has used his people as his primary vehicle for proclaiming his glory and working out his plan. This is what Ferguson was expressing. The church is at the center of the mission of God as his primary vehicle for advancing the kingdom and declaring the gospel—not as a corporation, but as a people.

Curiously, despite God's proclivity toward this means, the modern church relies little on his people to progress the gospel. We put significantly more faith in technology and programs, and expect little out of the members of our churches. Now don't get me wrong, I see the value in leveraging technology. Technology has been used by God from the arch to the Gutenberg printing press, and I am all for the strategic use of technology. But we should remember that God has made us in his image for a purpose. The greatest resource the church has is not its technology or its wealth. It is the people themselves, image bearers of God, purchased by the blood of Jesus, to be sent to proclaim the gospel through which they have been redeemed. When we understand the importance of community in the work of God, then we will begin to employ his greatest resource to that end.

With this in mind, I would like to suggest that there are three primary functions of the church for which community groups can and should be the vehicle. They are discipleship, pastoral care, and mission. Let's take a look at how community groups can transform the way we perform these functions of the church.

DISCIPLESHIP

> And Jesus came and said to them, "All authority in heaven and on
> earth has been given to me. Go therefore and make disciples of
> all nations, baptizing them in the name of the Father and of the
> Son and of the Holy Spirit, teaching them to observe all that I have
> commanded you. And behold, I am with you always, to the end of
> the age.[5]

Let's think about this responsibility to disciple the church, from pre-
conversion to "Well done, good and faithful servant."[6] This is a large
task that is going to take some thought. It is not easy to shepherd a
large flock toward maturity, and sadly, many large churches abdi-
cate their responsibility in this area. This is unfortunate because
although discipleship is hard work, it is also a joy to participate in the
redemptive work of God. Why would we abandon such a wonderful
responsibility? As we determine to be a church of disciples who make
disciples, we will find that we have been equipped for all such good
works and that the results will be worth the sweat and tears.

Discipleship is about trajectory. It is taking chaos and giving
it direction. Our goal is not a destination as if we could run people
through a program that spits out fully mature disciples. Rather, discipleship is about providing a means by which we begin to shepherd
people in the direction of maturity. Think of a stream rather than a
processing plant between two lakes. Discipleship classes and the like
can only be considered a booster shot within a greater strategy for
discipleship. This is because discipleship is a lifelong pursuit. When
developing a plan for discipleship within the church, it must be perpetual and built to accommodate the whole church.

In a very practical way, if the church is responsible for the discipleship of its members, then our strategy for discipleship must
be scalable and effective for the majority of the population of our
church. The graph below is a populations curve that represents the
people in your church. (Forgive me as I channel my inner nerd for
a second.) This curve comes from probability theory, which pre-
dicts how data clumps near the average, and is useful when trying
to understand populations of people. In this particular curve I am

plotting maturity versus number of people. We can expect, at least for a decent-sized church, that there will be a range of maturity within the body. Most will clump near some average, and there will be fewer that are exceptionally mature or exceptionally immature. Remember the old adage that 10 percent of the people do 90 percent of the work? Well, that not only drives your pastors nuts, it also lends anecdotal evidence to the chart below. Those ten percent are the leaders represented on the right side, while the new and nonbelievers are represented on the left.

Congregational Maturity Curve

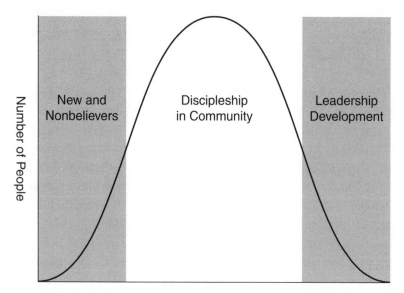

What this shows is that the majority of the people within your church will be within some average range of maturity, with fewer people at the extremes.

Hopefully you have a steady flow of new people in your church; in that case, the graph would simply shift to the right, but the shape would be relatively the same. You can see the difference in the modified figure below.

Congregational Maturity Curve Comparison

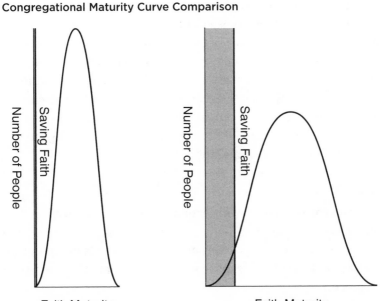

A church that is neither growing through conversion nor spiritual maturity will have a skinnier distribution. In other words, most of its members will have about the same level of maturity and will be content to stay there. You would see fewer immature people on the left because the church is not growing, and you would see fewer people on the right because the church is not maturing, indicating a lack of mission.

A missional church will see more people at the beginning of their walk with Jesus and therefore will spread out the distribution quite a bit. If that church is committed to developing leaders and spiritual growth, then it will again spread out the curve, as you will have more diversity in levels of maturity, but the shape remains the same. Certainly we should strive to see our church look like the figure on the right rather than the figure on the left, but notice the shape doesn't change and the bulk of your congregation is still in the center of the graph.

So what is the point? The point is that we can use this understanding of our congregation to build a discipleship strategy that best helps people grow in maturity. Oftentimes, having a different strategy for different populations within the church may be more effective than a one-size-fits-all strategy. Additionally, from the chart we see that the bulk of our people are in that average category. Therefore, our primary discipleship methodology must target that population if we are to effectively disciple the church. In other words, if we create a discipleship program that cannot efficiently and effectively disciple that center group, then we will not be successful in fulfilling the second half of the Great Commission.

Modes of Discipleship

So what type of strategy will accomplish this in an effective way? Churches spend countless hours conjuring up programs for discipleship. However, too often we rely on inferior methods for producing disciples and end up using too many resources for too little return in the process.

Let's step back for a moment and consider the methods we have for discipleship within the church. A disciple is defined broadly as a "learner." So what is the best way to help someone learn about Jesus and follow him? We have several modes of teaching at our disposal. Traditionally in our Western culture that is derived from a Greek system of learning, we consider three options: preaching, classes, and one-on-one mentoring.

Teaching Methods Comparison

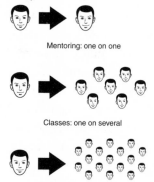

Mentoring: one on one

Classes: one on several

Preaching: one on many

For small populations, classes and mentoring have a great return and intimacy. The close interaction makes it simple to clearly articulate the material to be learned and elicit feedback. For large populations, however, these methods don't always scale very well. They have high resource input (in time and effort) to influence a small group of people.

Let's say you have a church of one hundred people and want everyone in the church to go through a membership class. If the class holds twenty-five people and is offered four times a year, then it will take a year to get the entire church that information. That assumes no new growth, but it allows you to teach your people a particular topic in a reasonable time frame. If, however, you have a larger church, say 250 people, and you factor in growth, say 10 percent, you start running into a problem. With only twenty-five new people a year (less than one every other week) it would take more than three years for everyone in that church to go through the membership class. Start at five hundred people and it jumps to ten years. Gone are the benefits of feedback and intimacy, and the time frame has become simply untenable, requiring a new strategy.

This is where community groups become a great vehicle for discipleship in the church. For large, growing churches, we need to leverage community more in conjunction with the preached Word. By leveraging one-on-many preaching with one-another discipleship in community, we get the advantage of clear teaching and the intimacy of community.

One-Another Teaching Method

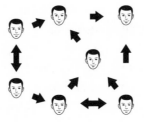

Community: one another

There is a reason that the New Testament is littered with commands to love, teach, admonish, and rebuke one another. By discipling one another we are not only learning, but also we are teaching the gospel. Instead of one teacher with many disciples, we create a community of disciples who are discipling one another. Teachers have long known that this is the best way to learn because you must know your subject well to teach it to others. In this way, as the Word is preached and then applied in community, we can disciple an entire population effectively and efficiently.

Taking what we learned from our population curve, we can build a strategy for discipleship that relies on community groups as the primary vehicle for discipleship of the bulk of the church. Then we can leverage methods like classes and mentoring to develop the smaller populations at the extremes of the curve. This allows us to focus our energy on discipling new believers and developing leaders.

It should be noted that these methods can overlap. I am not saying that you should never have classes targeted at the average member of the church or that you should not offer mentoring programs. But you can only put so much hope in such programs. Discipling the whole church will take a strategy that can incorporate the entire church. Thus, leveraging community groups for such a task is not only a reasonable expectation for the community of God, but it is also much more effective.

Transformation Cycle

Our goal in discipleship is to see the lives of our people transformed by the gospel. So how does transformation occur in the church? Of course, this is the work of the Holy Spirit in us, but nonetheless, Scripture consistently admonishes us to respond to the gospel as a part of that process. We are not passive participants in sanctification. We are called to be active in the process of our own spiritual growth and that of our brothers and sisters. Therefore, as the church we must consider how we are shepherding one another toward that sanctification in response to the expectations of Scripture.

Mars Hill has always leaned heavily on the pulpit. We are a

preaching church. But the Bible warns us not to be mere hearers of the Word. We need to be doers.[7] The danger of a church that relies heavily on the pulpit is that we can be lulled into being content that our people have heard the gospel day in and day out. James reminds us, however, that if our faith does not produce good works, then it is not faith at all.[8] The reason this is so important is that this "doing" testifies to the faith we have in addition to being the agent for the transformation of our lives. As we live out the gospel through the help of the Holy Spirit, we are being sanctified through that work. Curiously, though, many churches are content with the proclamation of the Word alone and do little to shepherd this "doing" of the Word.

Think of it like playing golf. I can study all the techniques and tricks that can be crammed into a magazine, and I can tell someone everything I've learned. But it doesn't make me a better golfer if I never swing a club. It's in the practice that one grows as a golfer. In the same way, it's through repentance and forgiveness that we grow in our discipleship of Jesus. It's through exercising patience and encouragement, rebuke and exhortation that we learn the deep truths of Scripture and how they apply to our lives.

With this in mind, we need to have a holistic approach to the way we "do" church. In many churches that I talk to, I see a disconnect between the gathered church on Sunday and the scattered church during the week. This disconnect weakens the church as a whole as energy and resources are not working together for the same goal.

At Mars Hill we use the analogy of the air war and the ground war. I know I just made some of you cringe, but stick with me for a second. First, it is an analogy, so relax. Second, it is biblical, so repent. Paul, James, and Peter all use the concept of war in regard to our sanctification.[9] With that in mind, we see the Sunday service as the air war, going first to proclaim the gospel to the believer and the world; we see the ground war as the ministries that do the hands-on ministry of the church to one another and to the lost. The preached Word prepares the hearts of the church to call one another to repentance on the ground. If you don't connect these two aspects of ministry for your church, you will waste much of your effort. When these are disconnected, the preached Word never gets a chance to get rooted in the hearts of people before it is assaulted by a different message from the ground war. Just as in war, this will lead to confusion and ultimately defeat. But if we can connect the two, we can bring a synergy to the ministry of the church that will bring about the transformation that we desire and expect through the work of the Holy Spirit.

We can call this the transformation cycle. The following diagram should help you understand what I am talking about.

Transformation Cycle

Sunday:
Attractional
Worship
Proclamation of Word

Product: Conviction

Community:
Incarnational
Application of Word

Product: Confession and
Repentance

In this diagram we basically identify the life of the church as two primary components (Sunday and community) that work in rhythm together to produce transformation.

SUNDAY

The first component is the gathering or Sunday experience. This is the attractional aspect of the church. "Attractional" simply means that we design our Sunday experience to draw people in to hear the gospel. We have contextualized music, aesthetics, and atmosphere to attract people to hear the Word.

During the gathering we proclaim the Word through preaching and respond in worship of Jesus. What this produces in the believer and nonbeliever alike is conviction through the Holy Spirit.

Nature: Attractional
Purpose: Corporate worship and proclamation of the Word
Product: Conviction

This in itself is progress for the gospel, but it should not end there. If we stop at conviction, we only produce a kind of worldly sorrow that leads to guilt but not change. We need a place for that conviction to lead to repentance, and that is where community groups come in. This is why they are so essential to the healthy functioning of the church.

COMMUNITY GROUPS

Community groups can be understood as the incarnational ministry of the church. As Timothy Lane and Paul Tripp note in *How People Change*, "Change is a community project."[10] Sanctification takes place as we live out the gospel together. This means that the conviction that comes from the proclamation of the Word leads to confession, repentance, and good works in community. It is then through this process that the seeds of the gospel take root and produce the fruit of the Spirit in a disciple's life. To be clear, this is not an event-to-event cycle. The Sunday gathering is an event, and community is a lifestyle lived out over the week.

Nature: Incarnational
Purpose: Living out the gospel in life together daily
Product: Confession and repentance

Putting these two together results in gospel-powered transformation. Some would argue that this is the actual church and would be willing to forgo the gathering of the church altogether. Let me raise an objection to that argument. While we lose repentance without community, we lose conviction without the consistent proclamation of the Word. God has ordained that the proclamation of the Word be an essential tool in the transformation of the believers' lives and for the conversion of souls.[11] Therefore, we should embrace both aspects of the transformation cycle and seek to bring them together for the making and maturing of disciples. Community groups are uniquely designed to be an effective and efficient method for that task.

PASTORAL CARE

One of the most disappointing conversations I have on a regular basis is the discussion of pastoral care within large churches. Sadly, most churches over a couple hundred members don't bother with pastoral care. Either that or they define pastoral care as a passive response to the most needy and ignore their responsibility to the bulk of the church.

When churches are small, a pastor can handle all the counseling and have a good handle on the health of the church. But as churches grow, this method isn't scalable and the system gradually breaks down. This leads to a body that is poorly shepherded and a church that neglects pastoral care for the average member. Either the leadership has put little thought into the ongoing care of the average member, or their system for pastoral care has been outgrown and they haven't taken the time to consider other ways to care for their flock. Instead, they focus on the Sunday gathering and provide counseling for the loudest needs (or they farm out their counseling to outside the church).

The assumption that most people are doing just fine leaves the average members and attendees basically to fend for themselves. Sadly, this is not close to reality. The church is a messy place full of sin and suffering. And not only does the church need pastoral care, but also this responsibility comes with leadership in the church. As a pastor, I take seriously the fact that I will give an account for the flock entrusted to me by Jesus.[12] That accountability does not diminish because your church grows. The solution is not to ignore the problem. The solution is to find better ways to care for the church.

Moses faced a similar problem when he was pastoring Israel.[13] As Israel grew, Moses got in the habit of sitting on the judgment seat and settling disputes for the whole nation. He would sit there day and night with no end to the counsel. While he was doing this, his stepfather Jethro visited and witnessed this chaos. Afterward, Jethro took Moses aside and gave him some advice. What he didn't say was that the system was not scalable, so ignore the needs of the people. What he told him to do was to entrust the oversight of the tribes to trustworthy men who had the capacity to oversee tens, hundreds, and thousands. What he was doing was establishing a system for pastoral care. This is known as the Jethro principle (we will look at this in more detail in chapter 8). We see the same thing in Acts as the disciples delegate care of the widows to deacons and establish elders to lead local congregations.[14] Central to this principle and important to our topic is that they found a way to ensure pastoral care for the entire church.

Therefore, you can see how a robust community group structure can provide a great means for pastoral care in the church. By entrusting delegated authority to community group leaders and leaders of leaders, you can ensure that every member is being cared for and is caring for others.

What this understanding implies is that community groups are not merely Bible studies or social groups, but they have a responsibility for the ongoing growth and care of the church. It also means that leaders must be trustworthy and qualified to care for the small flocks in their hands. When done well, this allows a church to grow to any size and still provide pastoral care for all its members. Not only is this beneficial for the health of the church, it will be very beneficial for the elders of the church when Jesus returns.

For Mars Hill Church this means that community groups are the primary vehicle for care in the church. We still provide one-on-one counseling for cases that require it, but we want the majority of that care to take place as the church loves one another and lives out the gospel together. To illustrate this, we use what we call the highway metaphor. That is to say, we want the majority of our people to be growing in their discipleship of Christ and sanctification through community, or the highway. Therefore, whenever possible, we shepherd people to community groups as the front line for care. We also provide special groups (called Redemption Groups) for people dealing with habitual sin or the effects of abuse, but these groups are temporary and designed to equip people with gospel truth and get them back on the highway.[15] Our counseling is done with the same intent—always striving to get people back into community for on-going sanctification. Our goal is to see 70 percent of pastoral care taking place in community, with the remaining 30 percent taking place in counseling or Redemption Groups. This ratio is illustrated by the following figure:

Pastoral Care Highway: Percentage of Care Methods

1:1 Counseling

Redemption Group

Community Group

Our goal is to be a people who wrestle daily with the gospel and its implications in our lives. We have been called and equipped through the Holy Spirit to minister to one another with the life-giving Word of God. We don't want to reestablish a priesthood of clergy that separates the ministry of the Word from ordinary life. Therefore, we leverage community groups as a place to wrestle with and repent of sin, and to walk with one another through trials and victories. In this way we are being the church to one another. There are over fifty verses in the New Testament alone on how we are to minister to one another, from loving one another to correcting and rebuking one another in love.[16] Community should be a place where the implications of the gospel are lived out in tangible and visible ways. And this should not occur only in the crisis moments of life, but it also should permeate the life of your community as you walk together.

MISSION

Last, but possibly most significant, is the role community groups play in the mission of the church. Ed Stetzer has said, "One of the reasons many believers are unengaged in mission is because they are unengaged in community."[17] The purpose of the church at the end of the day is to be an effective tool for the mission of God.[18] The church is not the purpose of the mission. Rather, God has been in the process of eliciting worship from his creation and redeeming mankind through his Son, Jesus. For his glory and our joy, he has, by his divine prerogative, chosen to use the church to accomplish this purpose.

This should not be a surprise. Since the beginning, God has always used his people to proclaim his glory. If you remember from chapter 1, this is why we were created. We were created to bear his image and proclaim his glory. This is backed up by the testimony of Scripture; God has continually called his people to be a "sign and instrument of his kingdom."[19] People have always been the greatest asset of the church.

Money is helpful and technology is great, but God has chosen to use his people to accomplish his mission. I say this to implore you not to try to shortchange this in your church. Leverage technology, but focus on getting your people on mission with God. They will do far more than you think. Our technology and our services will only reach those who are willing to darken the door of the church or tune in to our communication channels. The people of God, however, have relational connections to the people of our cities in all the nooks and crannies. They are connected to all the peoples that we are exhorted by Jesus to reach with the gospel.[20]

If this is the case, then we must employ the *whole* church in the mission of God. This is where community groups come into play. When the gospel is lived out in community, we find our identity in Jesus; we are compelled to worship God, love one another, and have compassion for the lost. As we are transformed by the gospel, our communities become places we want others to experience. We want our friends and neighbors to be transformed by Jesus, and they become a source of missional growth for the church. If we look again

at our transformation cycle, we now see two inputs for conversion—
the gathered and the scattered church.

Transformation Cycle with Missional Groups

Sunday:
Attractional
Worship
Proclamation of Word

Product: Conviction

Community:
Incarnational
Application of Word

Product: Confession and
Repentance

We know we have successfully made mature disciples when we
get to the place where people meet Jesus in our community groups.
You see, until we have disciples making disciples, we are still drink-
ing milk.[21] We are infants in our discipleship because we can't see
beyond our own saved skins. But when we get to the place where our
communities are making disciples and teaching them the Word of
God, we are accomplishing the Great Commission.

NUMBERS AND LEGACY

For me, understanding the importance of community groups within
the life of the church is about building the right legacy. Most churches
tend to measure their legacies by either numbers or effectiveness.
However, building a healthy church requires both objective and sub-

jective measurements. At the end of the day, success will not only be defined by how many people we reached with the gospel, but by the depth the gospel penetrated into their lives as well.

Subjective measurements can be difficult, but what doesn't lie is our response to adversity and trial. Shake a man, and you will see what spills out of his heart. Watch a community address sin and adversity, and you will see if the gospel has taken root in their lives. These are better measures of our success in creating disciples and advancing the kingdom. We cannot be content with large numbers in the gathered church without qualitative growth in our love and devotion to Jesus. We cannot be content until we see the ongoing sanctification of our churches as we are continually challenged to grow and exalt Christ in our lives.

Let me assure you, however, that I do see value in numbers. A common mistake of the "I got burned by a megachurch so I won't be anything like them" crowd is that they see large churches as somehow selling out to worldly success. Some churches have earned this skepticism, but it would be foolish to assume that all large churches are unfaithful. There is a biblical expectation that faithful churches will grow. God is in the business of growing his church.[22] Such aversion to large churches in general is a silly notion when we look at the biblical history of the church. Acts 2 tells us that the church began as a church of over three thousand people who met in homes daily.[23] This looks like a megachurch living out the gospel in community groups to me.

So, I don't have a problem with numbers. Each person who attends a service to see the gathered church worship and submit to the preached Word of God is glorious progress for the gospel. Those numbers are souls who are being washed by the water of the Word. Our goal ought to be to build the largest and deepest churches we can. I want our legacy to be one of transformation *and* growth.

As I mentioned earlier, James calls us to be doers of the Word and not just hearers.[24] Therefore, we must consistently strive for transformation in our lives and the lives of the people in our community. Don't be content with a legacy that looks back on your ministry and says, "Wow, they gathered a lot of people." Instead, strive for a legacy of transformation that will recall the life of your church as one that changed the lives of all who came into contact with it. Fight for the legacy of a church that changed the city within which it existed, and one that lifted up the name of Jesus to be worshiped and adored.

As we saw at the beginning of this chapter, Ferguson suggests that the church is at the center of the eternal purpose of God. Thus, we must leverage our most precious resource, the people of God, to that eternal purpose for the glory of God and the fame of Jesus. By establishing community groups as one of the primary ministries of the church, we can leverage the body of Christ for that mission. And when you take all of the ideas we have to help groups grow, nothing will bring life quicker than the tangible excitement of being used by God.

3

OWNERSHIP

BORROWED FAITH

Now that we have built a biblical foundation for community groups and understand their significance for the church, we have to ask how this leads to life in our groups. After all, having intellectual understanding does not necessitate change. That is because change occurs when, and only when, we take ownership of these principles and the mission of God saturates the church. As the people of God, we are the vehicle through which God is making his appeal to the world.[1] Within each believer is the potential for world transformation through the empowerment of the Holy Spirit.[2] When we awaken this truth in the body of Christ, we unleash the church.

I recently asked a couple, who I knew consistently attended church, about their convictions on a particular topic. It was not a tough question. I intended to find common ground for a light conversation. Their response was curious: "We believe whatever our pastor teaches." While I applaud their loyalty and trust in their pastor, this response was not a resounding expression of conviction.

Now, few evangelical churches would be satisfied with that level of belief (if it were a belief at all), yet this is the position that most churches take toward the mission of the church. Though they may be able to recite the mission statement, very few members have a deep conviction and ownership of it. In this chapter, we will explore the need to own the mission of your church and to instill that ownership within every member of the body.

DEFINING MISSION

What does it mean for a church to be missional? In the first chapter, we established the idea that we are created for the purpose of displaying and proclaiming the gospel through transformed lives in community. In the second chapter, we established the place and purpose of community within the church. Community groups provide a vehicle for discipleship, pastoral care, and mission toward the purpose of displaying the gospel to the world. In this chapter we will begin to focus more intently on the function of mission.

The church exists "that together [we] may with one voice glorify the God and Father of our Lord Jesus Christ."[3] Just as we exist as image bearers of God, so the church exists to reflect his goodness and to call people to worship him as we make disciples and proclaim the gospel.[4] Unfortunately, our view of the church can get so distorted that it seems as though God exists for the church. The mission of the church becomes to expand the church rather than to expand the worship of God.

When this happens, we create a church with a mission. The church is the sending agent and the mission is the active outworking of that church. Ed Stetzer, a leading missiologist in the church today, argues that this is a consistent historical mistake of the church.[5] To paraphrase Stetzer, missions should not be a hobby of the church. When we understand the mission of God, we realize that it is the *mission* that has a *church*, not the other way around. God has a mission—to call people to worship and exalt the Son through the work of the Holy Spirit. God is the sending agent and the church is the active outworking of the mission.

We cannot be content with the status quo of passive participation in the work of the church. The work of the church *is* the mission of God. In response to the grace we have received, we get to share the good news and radical truth of Jesus and what he has done.[6] It is, therefore, the great joy of the Christian to be an active part of that mission, proclaiming the gospel and living out its redeeming truth for the fame of Jesus. Alan Hirsch articulates the mission of the people of God as the "mission of every believer into every sphere and domain of society."[7] As God's ambassadors on his mission, we get to share the gospel in every nook and cranny of the city. That is what it means to be missional: to be on mission with God.

Because the terms *mission* and *missional* are used in so many ways these days, we cannot even begin to call the church to missional thinking without first defining the term. Therefore, my definition of *missional* is "to participate in the mission of God as a response to the gospel through proclamation and practice."

The modern conversation regarding the missional church can be traced back to a conference of the International Missionary Council at Willingen, Germany, in 1952, which stated "there is no participation in Christ without participation in his mission to the world."[8] Sadly, this statement may alienate much of Christendom. Yet, it clearly reflects the expectation that Jesus gave the church: to go and make disciples. As we share the gospel of Christ and reflect its redeeming power in our lives, we get to participate with God as he gathers more disciples to himself. We get to be a part of the gospel work for which we were born.

Therefore, we must have a clear picture of what it means to participate in the mission of God. In sum, we are to proclaim the truth of Jesus Christ in word and action, not as pretentious judges intent on proving the stereotypes assigned to Christians that already taint the culture against the church, but as believers who remember what it was like to be lost. Peter reminds us that once we were lost, once we were isolated and not a people, once we had not received mercy; but now, through Jesus, we have been found.[9] To be on mission with Jesus is to remember that we were plucked from death through the grace of Christ. It was not our astute theology that saved us. We were once heretics, rebels, and heathens who hated God until he turned his face toward us. Therefore, our verbal proclamation of the truth of Christ must first be inspired by compassion—to engage our neighbors in a discourse and say, "I know what you are looking for; I was once there looking for it too, and I found the answer in Jesus."

I was talking with one of my leaders after he had another long conversation with a gentleman who had been frequenting Mars Hill for the past six months. This man had attended men's retreats and multiple services each Sunday. Many of us had talked with him and shared the gospel with him. We had seen various levels of conviction and remorse but little repentance, as he was unwilling to put his faith in Christ. This leader was exasperated after his latest multiple-hour conversation. He was frustrated with the tears that didn't lead to change. He was almost angry that our friend still would not confess Jesus as Lord.

Why do we raise our voice when talking to someone who is blind? They aren't deaf; they just cannot see. Yet I completely sympathize with my friend's response. All the pieces had come together for this guy, yet he refused to believe. He could not argue anymore against the truth of Jesus's claims. Every challenge had been met, every argument countered, and even his heart seemed to be pierced by the reality of his sin. Yet he remained blind; his will was still in opposition to the truth of God. And therein lies the rub. A blind man will not see, no matter how hard or loud you tell him. We cannot fault a man for being blind and demand him to see. We can only pray that Jesus would give him sight and thank Jesus for healing our own blindness.

When I remember the grace that brought me to the cross, I respond with compassion. When I am focused on my confidence in my theology, I respond with indignation. The former is better. Engaging people where they are and pointing them to Jesus is our great commission and joy and is part of what it means to be missional. It is the practical outworking of worshiping our God and wanting more people to worship him.

The second half of that equation—proclaiming the truth of Jesus Christ in word and action—is the response to the gospel in practice. This is the practical and tangible extension of grace to our neighbors as a reflection of the grace we have received. Because God has so loved us, we are free to love others.[10] Jesus rebukes religious people who see the culture's needs and do nothing to meet them.[11] Too often, the people of God justify ignoring the needs of others. We offer our sympathy and prayers, but we don't actually pray nor do we try to help. We assume it is someone else's responsibility. Others just pretend the problems don't exist. We hide behind ignorance. We don't know what the needs are in our community because we don't want to know.

As a missional church being reconciled to God and to one another, we are a missional people who get to practically love others. We do this not just by supporting programs but also by looking people in the eyes and being their friends. James tells us that faith without works is dead.[12] He calls us to be doers and not merely hearers.[13] He says that true religion cares for widows and orphans.[14]

We cannot believe the gospel without being moved to action by it. If we believe that Jesus is the light of the world, if we believe that he and he alone is worthy of worship, then we will be compelled to join in with God on mission. Jesus says the two greatest commandments are to love God and love our neighbor. If we are not concerned with advancing the kingdom of God by sharing the gospel through our lives, then we don't love either.

As we see that the mission of God must be worked out in proclamation and practice, we begin to grasp what it means to be missional beyond cool shirts and hip hair. The essence of mission is the compassionate heart of God. When our hearts beat in rhythm with his, we begin to see his mission and are ready to take ownership of it.

IT'S A RENTAL

The technical definition of ownership is to take possession of or to possess something. This is the framework that we will use for our definition of ownership. To own an ideology, vision, or mission is to take possession of it, to make it your own. It is to internalize it to the point where not only can you reiterate it, but also you can teach it, defend it, and live it.

It was a perfect day for the beach, and my new bride and I had the top down in a fun but gutless Mustang. My faith in the directions our host had given us was waning, but I was still having a good time. We had left the main track miles ago and were tearing down a dirt road riddled with potholes. There was a sign saying something about four-wheel drive a few clicks back, but I didn't bother getting the details. My wife began to get nervous about our adventure and asked if we should be taking a Mustang on a road like this. Without hesitation, I uttered those three little words that put our minds at ease and that have been used by most of us at one time or another to justify the reckless disregard for vehicle degradation:"It's a rental."

It's amazing how differently we treat things that we own versus rent. Ownership gives us a sense of responsibility and care. It is ours, and in some way it reflects who we are, so we take care of it.

For several years I drove an old Buick Park Avenue that my wife and I had bought from her grandfather. It was hot beige with a beige interior. Not exactly the ride of choice for a young man, but it was mine. It was not nearly as nice as the gutless Mustang we rented on our honeymoon, yet I treated it much better. My treatment of a car reflects my level of ownership more than it reflects the value of the car itself.

In the same way, when it comes to the mission of the church, our responses reflect our ownership more than any other aspect of the mission. Our churches may have a clear, innovative, Holy Spirit–inspired vision for how God is calling us to proclaim his kingdom,[15] but if we collectively have no ownership of that mission, we will be hard pressed to achieve anything. God is not limited in accomplishing his plans by our lack of ownership, but he has chosen, for his glory and our joy, to employ us in his work, and I don't want to miss out on that.

Now, if owning a car makes you more careful when driving it, owning an idea makes you more passionate when sharing it. To test this theory, go to your favorite coffee shop or pancake house and offer your opinion on the most recent presidential election. You will soon discover who owns the vision and ideologies that each candidate represented. You will also get a pretty clear idea of who was not impressed with either candidate, at least not to the point of owning their ideals.

The folks who own the vision of their candidate can articulate it well and are intent on convincing others of the merits of their position. They may have attended rallies and bought bumper stickers and undoubtedly had a lawn sign. Ownership and passion for those ideals drove them to live differently, to join the cause. Those who did not own the vision of any particular candidate will most likely finish eating their pancakes. They couldn't care less and probably will not have a strong opinion until they are personally affected, in a positive or negative manner, by those ideas. They don't own them and therefore have no passion for them.

The same principle applies to your ownership of the mission within the church. Ownership inspires passion and leads to action. Yet, for the Christian, ownership does not come from believing in a good idea but from faith in the good news. Our ability to own comes from the fact that we *are owned* by Christ.[16] We inherit ownership from our Father. Thus, we don't need to manufacture ownership as much as we need to awaken the church to the reality that this is our mission. We are agents of the king.[17] It is already ours; we need only to exercise that ownership.

So what is the mission of your church? Can you articulate it? Does it instill passion in you that causes you to live your life differently? How about the rest of your church? Do your church members display passion and ownership of the mission, or do they finish their pancakes?

SATURATED OWNERSHIP

My wife and I have owned two homes in our life. The first thing we do when we buy a home is paint. And just to be clear, when I say "we" paint, I generally mean that she picks out the colors and I paint. This ritual is a way for us to make the house our own. There is no law that makes us paint the house or take care of it. Rather, this is our response to ownership. Because I own it, it's my responsibility to maintain it and improve it toward some semblance of its intended glory.

In contrast, I have never painted an apartment. It is not mine. When something breaks, it is the landlord's responsibility to fix it. This is a picture of many of our churches today. Leaders have become landlords of a rented mission.

I have observed, even in the most articulate and missional churches, a disparity in ownership of the mission between the leadership of the church and the church itself. While leaders of the church may be passionate and driven toward the goals set out by their mission, they often face a congregation that is passive or even apathetic. The church lacks ownership. They have not internalized the mission to the point of it becoming their own. You could say that they haven't painted the walls.

If we want to accomplish the mission of the church, then we need to get brushes in every hand. We need to make sure that ownership does not reside only in the elders and pastors of the church, but is instead shared by every member. Ownership needs to permeate every fiber of the church as a sponge that is saturated with water. No matter where you touch it, the sponge releases a flood of power. When the church is saturated in the mission of God, from the preacher to the janitor, the mission overflows out of everywhere. Lives are changed through the witness of the church because no matter who you encounter, a flood of the gospel is released. Don't just tell your church what to do; remind them of who they are and what Christ has done. Inspire them to take ownership of the mission that God has graciously given to them.

AGREEMENT VS. OWNERSHIP

So when you think about your church, is it the church you attend or is it *your* church? Let me challenge you with what may not be an obvious statement. Agreement does not equal ownership. "I like what *you* are doing" is dramatically different than "I believe in what *we* are doing."

When I suggested earlier that the church does not own the mission, I am not saying that they disagree with it. Agreement simply means that people like the idea of the mission and are excited about someone at the church carrying it out. They may not, and probably don't, see themselves as the church, or at least not the part of the church that lives out the mission. This manifests in casual attendance and participation in programs and events that serve their needs but don't require anything of them. Agreement can even involve serving in various ministries if the bar is low enough; but if the mission is not owned, if it is not internalized within the people, then they will not take risks for the sake of the gospel. They won't risk comfort, time, money, or self-interest for the mission to see Jesus glorified.

Our churches are filled with people who agree with the mission but do not own it. Ownership is marked by joy-filled sacrifice that sees kingdom work as a "get to" because of what Christ has done, rather than a "got to" out of Christian duty. Ownership looks like people serving the church and the city with a passion for the gospel. It looks like people cheerfully and sacrificially giving out of love for Jesus to see the work of the gospel move forward. Ownership looks like people participating in the messiness of community and being inconvenienced for the sake of another's sanctification. If you want to test your church's ownership level, check these three markers:

1. How many people serve? Do we consistently lack volunteers in children's ministry, hospitality, and other service areas?
2. How many people give to the church? What percentage of our attendance actually contributes financially to the gospel's advancing?
3. How many people are committed in community? Do we have a culture that lives out its faith together?

The data you find can be discouraging, but we need to be honest about the level of ownership within our churches if we want to correct the problem and lead our churches to health.

Addressing the issue of ownership won't guarantee missional community. But when coupled with hearts moved by the grace of God, the gospel becomes preeminent in our lives and motivations. We will sacrifice the nonessentials for the sake of the mission. Identifying areas where we lack ownership exposes heart failure and gospel distortions. By speaking the gospel to one another, we will be reminded of the love God has poured out on us, and we can call one another to the mission for the sake of the gospel and the glory of Christ.

A great illustration of this concept is in the movie *Miracle*.[18] Coach Herb Brooks is putting together the US Olympic hockey team from a group of college players. Molding these rivals into a single team proves to be a challenge as each player still identifies himself with his college team. Coach Brooks makes this point by asking each player his name and for whom he plays. The answer from one player is, "Rob McClanahan. St. Paul, Minnesota." Asked who he plays for, the response is, "I play for you, here at the U." He asks the same question of a few other players, and after they all miss the point, he sends them to the line to skate sprints.

This issue persists through their ups and downs until the movie builds to the climax. As the team is preparing to face the impossible task of defeating the Russian juggernaut, the light turns on for one of the players. The exchange goes like this:

> Mike Eruzione: "Mike Eruzione! Winthrop, Massachusetts!"
> Herb Brooks: "Who do you play for?"
> Mike Eruzione: "I play for the United States of America!"

In this instant everything changed. This was the moment that ownership for the mission took place. Mike was no longer just agreeing with the mission to win a gold medal for the United States; he now owned it. He wasn't borrowing it from Coach Brooks anymore.

I long for the day when the light goes on for the members of our churches, when we realize that we get to participate in the mission of God, and when we stop borrowing and start owning the mission for ourselves. As disciples of Christ, we are too easily content with agreement in our own lives and the lives of our brothers and sisters in Christ. Let's call one another to ownership and see how that changes everything.

INSPIRING OWNERSHIP

So how do we inspire ownership? I have been chasing the answer to this question since I began leading community groups. I have had some success, but I have also made plenty of mistakes in this area. I have rebuked people for their lack of passion, and I have encouraged people just to take baby steps. I have appealed to my leaders' sense of duty and have stoked their competitive fires. I have set goals and objectives and have put accountability structures in place. And in the end, each of these tactics had differing measures of success but very little sustainability.

What went wrong? It was like trying to inspire a painter with a tube of paint. It is not the paint that is inspiring—it is the sunset.

If you want to inspire people to the mission of God, you must lift up the Son. When we grasp the glory of Jesus, it becomes the sustaining inspiration that transforms life. Isaiah was inspired by seeing Jesus in the temple.[19] Peter was inspired by seeing Jesus after his resurrection.[20] Paul was inspired when he encountered Jesus on the road to Damascus.[21] These men were changed when they saw the glory of Jesus. His mission became their mission. His glory was enough to change everything.

Our apathy toward the mission of God is not because of a lack of knowing what to do. It is our blindness to his glory and grace that keeps us satisfied with nominal Christianity. If you want to light a fire under your church for the mission, don't simply trot out your goals; lift up Jesus. When we see him in his power and are overcome by his love, we are joyfully compelled to respond to his call to make disciples. We are energized to reach the lost and help the weak. We are inspired to worship and to call the lost to his feet.

Peter reminds us in his first letter that we are people called to the mission of God to worship Jesus and to see people know and worship him.[22] Because Jesus has redeemed us and reconciled us to the Father, we get to live in such a way that shows his great mercy and grace. His love is inspiration enough for us to live lives that reflect the goodness and mercy of God and ultimately to draw people to Christ: that "they may see your good deeds and glorify God."[23] We will draw this out in later chapters, but notice here that the purpose of living honorable lives is to draw people to worship God. Obedience motivated by law or fear is religion. Obedience inspired by love is missional.

PROFIT SHARING

Now let's look at some things that encourage ownership. First, when we give people the opportunity to participate in the mission, ownership increases. Consider, for example, how profit sharing motivates a corporation's employees. Employees who get to share in the company's profits are motivated to produce more and reduce cost. For any for-profit company, profit is the mission; by sharing profits, they invite their employees to own the mission.

One profit-sharing employee told me how he and his officemates would share one stapler and reuse misprinted paper by turning it over and making a recycled notepad. If they saw a coworker being wasteful, they confronted the coworker with "encouragement" to find more efficient ways to work. How profound! The company was self-regulating. The boss didn't have to micromanage the floor because employees took ownership and inspired ownership in their coworkers.

Now imagine if we could do that in the church. It should be pretty easy. Our "product" is much better. The "profit," the exaltation of Jesus, is more fulfilling. And the self-regulation, loving one another, is significantly more enjoyable.

When we challenge the body (community groups) to contextual-ize their groups and engage their culture to reach the lost, we share with them the joy of the ministry. We give them the opportunity to see the Holy Spirit transform lives and save people. That is worth sharing a stapler for. When we share in the work and joy of ministry, we will begin to sacrifice and take risks for the gospel. We will live differently to increase the "profits," the redeemed lives of our cities.

PROGRAM ERROR

Unfortunately, overprogramming often smothers the opportunity for profit sharing. It kills ownership. I cannot stand the consumer mentality in the church today, and I am sure we all can agree on this point. It is just too bad that we created it.

I know that we like to think this mentality in the church is some infection that we caught while bearing our crosses in the world. But let us be frank for a moment—how could our church not have a consumer mentality? We expect very little from the disciples of Jesus in our body. When someone is depressed, we send them to a church counselor. When our children need to learn about Jesus, we send them to Sunday school. When someone wants to grow in Christ, we sign him or her up for a mentor program. When I cannot pay my rent,

I submit a benevolence request. If I want someone to hear the gospel, I invite them to Sunday service.

You get where I am going. We have so programmed the church to function as a well-oiled machine that we leave no room for Christians to be Christians. Are not these the functions of the church, as in the people of God, rather than the church, the institution? Seriously, what is left for the disciple of Christ to do? As Hirsch points out, "We have created passivity through the way we have done church."[24] We think we are helping by providing every imaginable service, but instead we are robbing the church of the joy of living out their faith and imaging God through encouragement, prayer, generosity, and witness.

Most celebrities spend their whole lives wanting attention and then complain they can't go to the grocery store. We spend our whole lives creating ministries to serve people and then complain that they want to be served. What if we took a different approach? What if we expected the church to love and serve one another rather than doing it all for them?

At the end of the day, people like to be needed. If we do not use a part of our body, it atrophies and becomes useless. In some cases it can even die. As Paul says, we cannot say that we do not need any part of our body.[25] When we do, it hurts the whole church. In light of this, we need to be strategic about the programs we offer and consider how they are helping or hindering our people from being disciples. Not all programs are bad, but every program either helps or hinders ownership. Therefore, we need to be wise about what opportunities we take from the body when we meet needs that could be met in community.

LEADING FROM THE EDGE

Another way to foster ownership is to allow people to lead from the edge. The idea is simply that you allow your people on the front lines to make decisions instead of the decision always coming from the top.[26] Like profit sharing, this instills ownership. By giving people more responsibility, they take more ownership of the quality and product. On the one hand, if a worker is asked to merely follow orders, he is less apt to care about the final product as long as his check clears. On the other hand, when we give people responsibility and freedom to develop the best product, they create better ways to do their jobs and innovate to increase profits.

When I worked as a project manager for a structural engineering firm, my job was to design the building and come in under budget. How I accomplished that was up to me. It was a lot of responsibility, but I also had the freedom to succeed. In order to reduce cost while still providing a quality design, I wrote programs, designed spread-sheets, and developed processes to work faster and more precisely. I researched new programs to increase productivity. I innovated because I owned the mission to design the best building for the lowest cost.

Think what could happen if we built our community groups with the freedom to contextualize and express community in whatever way best reaches the individual neighborhood of that group, taking the gospel into "every sphere and domain of society."[27] What unique expressions of community could be possible if we entrusted our church with the mission?

RAISING EXPECTATIONS

Ownership also increases when we raise expectations. It is time to swim upstream when it comes to expectations, especially in regard to leadership. When it comes to community group leader recruit-ment and development, a popular philosophy that propagates in the small group world is that anyone with a pulse can lead a com-munity group. Now, on one hand, I understand the roots of this philosophy. Developing a thriving small group ministry is difficult, and finding leaders is a consistent pain point in most small group ministries. In order to address the lack of leaders, we lower the expectations in hopes of recruiting lower-hanging fruit. We build turnkey programs that require little from a leader except reading questions from a sheet of paper. This is another example of how we rob people of ownership. Expect little and you will get exactly what you expected.

Groups led by leaders who do not own the mission are at best social gatherings and at worst stagnant pools of pop therapy and gossip. Even when we take the best of these possible outcomes, we have to face the reality that there are plenty of alternative sources for social interaction that are better than a poorly led group. The fact is, when we lower the expectations for the leaders, we lower the expectations for our groups. At some point, you are merely organizing people into measurable units for purposes of management, and they have little spiritual value. This does not inspire ownership, and it certainly does not give life.

Alternatively, when we raise expectations, God's people have a way of rising to the occasion—not by their bootstraps, but by a renewed sense of dependence on the Spirit. As we are stretched beyond our capacities, we realize that we cannot do what God has called us to unless we abide in Jesus and trust him to use us for his glory. Call your leaders to live like this, and you will create a culture of Holy Spirit–dependent believers who accomplish more for the kingdom than they ever thought possible.

As we have raised the expectations for community groups and leaders at Mars Hill, we have seen a dramatic effect. The community group ministry was transformed into a fertile field for missional activity and leadership development. Once marked by contentment and management, we started to see men rise up to become pastors and church planters. As they leaned into the Spirit, their passion for the gospel and willingness to walk in faith increased tremendously. Instead of being content with agreeing with the mission of the church, they have taken ownership and trust that God can use them to advance the gospel. Baristas, engineers, programmers, contractors, architects, and others have taken ownership of the mission and have become pastors leading God's people.

As the priesthood of believers indwelt with the Holy Spirit, we all have the opportunity to participate in God's redemptive plan for our blocks, our neighborhoods, and our cities. Because our identities are secure in Christ, we can live with boldness for Jesus. And as we live in faith on mission for him, we can trust that he will be with us for every step.[28]

That is a picture of a community group that will be a source of life. It will be a place of discipleship, worship, and mission. When leaders take ownership, they inspire those around them, resulting in community groups who worship Jesus, love one another, and participate in the mission of God. There are no alternatives to community that can breathe that kind of life into your soul.

BITE-SIZED MISSION

Finally, to inspire ownership, you must also cast a vision that is accessible. Even churches that see themselves as missional often alienate the body by casting a vision that is out of reach for the average member. That is not to say that we should not have a God-sized vision. Rather, we must learn to communicate the vision and mission in clear terms that inspire and invite the entire church into participation. This starts with believing the foundational principles that we established in the first two chapters and then providing opportunities for everyone to participate in the mission.

For example, if God has called you to transform your city, consider how the average member will understand his or her role in that mission. If I don't have a microphone, a radio show, a blog, or a website, how am I going to affect the entire city? A vision too big to grasp at the individual level can leave the church feeling insignificant in the mission of God. We steal the joy of our people when they have no opportunity to own the mission and to image Jesus.

Again, transforming your city is a fine vision. It just needs to be broken down into bite-sized pieces so that everyone understands how participation contributes to this greater goal. (We will discuss how we do this at Mars Hill in chapter 5.) When you are casting vision, think bite sized. Articulate the greater vision and then break it down so that it is accessible to everyone. God has made us all parts of one body for the purpose of giving him glory through the exaltation of Jesus. Helping people to see their parts in such a great mission will inspire ownership in the mission. Ownership will in turn inspire innovation and creativity and make the vision God has given your church achievable.

COMMUNITY OWNERSHIP

If we want to be a missional church that sees the lives in our cities transformed by the gospel, we must foster a holy discontentment with the status quo and resist apathy toward God's mission. Compelled by the grace of God manifested in the atoning work of Jesus on the cross and his resurrection, we can take ownership of proclaiming the truth of the gospel and living it out in community.

> Restore to me the joy of your salvation,
> and uphold me with a willing spirit.
> Then I will teach transgressors your ways,
> and sinners will return to you.[29]

Community groups offer us the most tangible opportunity to call people to the mission of God. If we can inspire the communities of believers in our churches to own the mission to see Jesus's name exalted, then we can make a lasting impact for the kingdom of God. Hirsch makes the observation that every revival in history has been a recovery of the "people of God being the people of God."[30] It is a reawakening of who we are in Christ and taking ownership of his mission. Give your people opportunities to be the most palpable expression of the gospel within the church. When we ourselves are transformed by the gospel, we will believe it, live it, and own it.

HEALTH PLAN: REDEFINING COMMUNITY GROUPS

CONVICTION VS. PRAGMATISM

Now that we have established the building blocks for life-giving community groups, it is time to consider the practical outworking of community that is built on that foundation. This section takes the theological and philosophical convictions that we discussed in the previous section and applies them to the real experience of living life together for the fame of Jesus. This is the key to sustaining life in your small groups.

As we transition from the foundational principles of community to the outworking in community groups, I want to emphasize the importance of building from these convictions. Practical theology is very popular in the church today, and rightfully so. Our theology should affect the way we live. Because we are chosen, holy, and beloved, we can live lives of compassion, humility, meekness, patience, and forgiveness.[1] Our understanding of the atonement, for example, should change how we parent as we pursue and forgive when our children rebel, how we interact with our spouses as we lay down our lives to love each other, and how we conduct ourselves as employees as we submit to and respect authority. Practical theology states that our theology determines our praxis.

This emphasis on the practical outworking of theology can lead to error, however, when we get theology and praxis inverted. When our experiences determine our theological convictions, we have become pragmatists, and not in a good way. That is not to say that pragmatism must be avoided. At the end of the day, what we call people to must be attainable and practical. Life is not theoretical. Our expectations for community are achievable with the help of the Holy Spirit as we abide in Christ. However, pragmatism does not determine the goal. Biblical convictions set the goal, and then we can work out the practical implications. Practical arguments are valid when they don't require you to alter your conviction and instead help you attain it.

Unfortunately, most small group ministries I come across while consulting have been developed primarily out of pragmatism rather than conviction. That is, often they have been built from a perspective of what will work rather than from a vision of what Jesus has done. The problem with starting from pragmatism is that it approaches solutions with preconceived limitations. It does not question the validity of those limitations but seeks only to accommodate them. This lowers our expectations of what God can do in and through community and leaves no room for the supernatural work of the Holy Spirit. I want you to question the limitations that you have accepted in the past for community in your church. Work around those that are valid and develop community that breaks through those that are illegitimate.

Another concern I have with starting from pragmatism is that it causes us to accommodate the limitations of apathy, cultural priorities, and sin rather than calling people to a passion for Jesus, God-centeredness, and holiness are that anchored in the power of the resurrection. Pragmatism says you should not expect much of people. It tells us to lower the bar and find ways to spoon-feed some God into their busy lives. That, however, is not the gospel.

Jesus's practical experience with Peter and the disciples could not have given him much hope that they would be able to take the gospel to the ends of the earth. Yet he did not accept their limitations nor lower his expectations. He called them to make disciples from Jerusalem and beyond.

My encouragement to you, whether you are a pastor or a member in community, is to live out of your convictions and faith. Because we have been redeemed, made new, and given the Holy Spirit, we get to share the good news of Jesus. Don't give up on your convictions and settle for pragmatism. Keep this in mind as we start to work through the practical steps of building community groups within your church in the next section.

DEPENDENCE ON THE HOLY SPIRIT

As we move toward strategy and application, now is a good time to remind ourselves that our greatest ally in advancing the kingdom is not a good strategy but the empowerment of the Holy Spirit. As you build community in your church, begin with prayer. Pray at least as much as you create spreadsheets. Pray for God to move and use you and the men and women of your church. He promises to respond for the fame of the Father.

Allow me to paraphrase John Piper from a lecture he gave on prayer.[2] He compared prayer to being in the middle of war and being given a walkie-talkie with a direct line to the general. Everything we need to fight and win the war is right at our fingertips. The problem is that we fail to see the war, thinking we are in a time of peace. If there is no war, then the walkie-talkie and the promises of support are not necessary. Piper summed up our use of prayer by saying that "we have turned our wartime radio into a domestic intercom." When I talk of living out of conviction, one area in my life and the life of the church that I see needs quite a bit of work is dependence on prayer and the work of the Holy Spirit. Just as Piper and 1 Peter note, we are in a time of war—not a war against the culture, but a war for our souls against the Evil One who wants to destroy us. We need to convert our intercoms back into wartime radios.

As a recovering engineer, I am good at building systems and developing foolproof plans. The problem is that they are often Spirit-proof as well. We can easily put so much faith in our programs and systems that we forget that it is God who brings the harvest. We sow and water but he makes it grow. As you use the ideas in this book to develop your own systems and programs, remember to do nothing without prayer and supplication and dependence on the Holy Spirit.

4

COMMUNITY

CONTROL-ALT-DELETE

In the last section we built a foundation for community, establishing a biblical conviction for the necessity of community as an expression of the image of God that has been restored through the cross. We determined the importance of community within the ecclesiology of the church and the importance of ownership related to the mission of God. Now I want to turn our attention to community groups themselves.

What are community groups in light of these convictions? At this point I want us to be able to clean the slate and rebuild our understanding of community groups on these principles and convictions. Our previous experiences in small groups can limit our imagination of what community can be. So let's dream for a minute that we never sat in that uncomfortable circle and answered icebreaker questions. How would we live in community if we started from scratch? What would be different about community built upon the foundation we laid in the previous chapters?

The purpose of this chapter is to paint a clearer picture of what community inspired by the Holy Spirit can look like. I want to challenge you to think differently about what community groups are and how they might manifest in your church. This is an exercise in how we view community and how we define it. I want your picture of community groups to be bigger and your expectation of what God might do through them to be greater.

When attempting to appreciate art, we often need to look at the piece from different angles. Understanding the intent of the artist requires not only understanding the piece itself but also knowing how it exists in history and context. My hope is that as we take a look at community groups from new angles, God would reveal more to us about his expectations for community. Let your appreciation for this gift grow. Hit control-alt-delete on your default picture of small groups, and let's start looking at them differently.

VISION VS. REACTION

As we begin, we want to be visionary rather than reactionary. We want to develop a clear vision for community groups from our convictions and build communities toward that goal. In other words, let the vision determine the expressions of community.

This seems like a simple concept, but most community group ministries are built in reaction to a particular need of the church. For example, if the pastoral care is lacking within the church, then groups often become care focused. After all, addressing acute needs in the church through community groups is an effective strategy. Here is the problem: experience shows that when community groups are designed around a particular need, they often fail to adjust when those needs change.

For example: A new church plant is drawing in a young, unchurched congregation. Being small, the need for fellowship and mission is satisfied at the congregational level. The highest need at the community level is theological understanding. In this case, the reactionary strategy is to build groups which are predominantly Bible studies in order to meet the acute need of the church at this time. This is perfectly fine for now, but what happens when the church grows? When fellowship and mission can no longer be done effectively as the corporate church, community groups need to adapt. When this doesn't happen, people start to feel disconnected from the church, and they begin to feel like an audience rather than members of a family. Mission becomes something the church (as an institution) does rather than what the people live out. You end up with members of the church who are biblically astute but don't apply their knowledge to loving one another or reaching the lost.

This is why it is important to start with a vision and build communities that align with it. Having a bigger picture of where you are going and what God wants for your church will allow you to adapt to acute needs while at the same time help you build more well-rounded community from the start. Moreover, if we begin with a picture of community that is formed out of the image of God and who we are in light of the cross, then we are sure to meet the particular needs of the church. This will provide transformational community at every stage of growth and will keep us from getting stuck on one particular need.

PRODUCT VS. PURPOSE

In order to have a vision for community, we need to understand the purpose of community. In my experience with community group ministry, I have heard many purposes for joining community groups, including but not limited to: belonging, making big church feel small, learning the Bible, pastoral care, fellowship, friends, closing the back door of the church, evangelism, and so on. Each of these purposes has merit and can be argued as essential to the church. I would suggest, however, that these "purposes" are in fact the product of community rather than its ultimate goal.

Why is this significant? Let me give you an example. When I was playing basketball in junior high, I went into the game off the bench as we were inbounding the ball. As I came off a screen, I found myself wide open under the basket. My teammate passed me the ball and I made an easy layup. The only problem: we were lined up under our opponent's basket. The point: it is increasingly difficult to score points for your team when you are aiming at the wrong basket. In the case of the church, our goal is to produce disciples of Jesus who worship him and exalt his name. If we aim at a product such as belonging as the purpose of community, we can achieve that goal without pointing to Jesus.

When retaining people becomes our goal, we inadvertently communicate that our purpose is to grow the church rather than glorify God. We become more interested in building the church rather than advancing the kingdom. We lift up the church rather than the name of Jesus.

As well, when fellowship, care, or belonging becomes the focus of our communities, we elevate people and their needs over the kingdom. In doing so, we create people who begin to believe the purpose of the church is to meet their needs. In essence, we create consumers.

Jesus tells us that we know a tree by its fruit and that a bad tree cannot produce good fruit.[1] If we produce disciples who are navel-gazers or are obsessed with the growth of the church at the expense of the gospel, then the tree is bad. Trying harder won't make it produce fruit. We need a healthy tree. Every time we elevate the fruit of ministry above the purpose to glorify God, we turn the fruit into an idol. The fruit becomes our focus and we settle for less than Christ glorified. As C. S. Lewis has said, "We are far too easily pleased."[2] Lewis was observing our propensity to settle for sin and its false promises.

More acceptable but no more futile is being satisfied with the peripheral blessings of God rather than enjoying God himself. Man has always had a bent toward worshiping created things rather than the Creator.[3] This is the definition of idolatry. We must, therefore, be careful that we do not inadvertently encourage one another to seek the blessing rather than the Author of the blessing by making the product of community its purpose.

At the end of the day, our purpose in community is to receive the grace of God and respond by imaging him and lifting up the name of Jesus. As we discussed in chapter 2, if community is about imaging God for his renown and his worship, then community groups must be in the business of creating disciples. In Pastor Bill Clem's forthcoming book *Disciple*, he rightly describes Jesus as the prototypical image bearer living a life devoted to the Father's work and accomplishing that work through the empowerment of the Holy Spirit. Jesus was more than an example, securing our redemption through his death and resurrection, yet he provides a picture of what we could be as disciples who walk in the Spirit. Additionally, by building a disciple-making movement, Jesus becomes not just our example of being a disciple, but he is also our example for being a disciple maker. Jesus left a legacy of people transformed by his presence even centuries after he ascended. In this way he provides a picture of a church that is committed to being disciples who make disciples.[4] Using Jesus's life as our template, Clem identifies four defining characteristics of a disciple that emerge from being image bearers of God: finding our identity in Jesus, worshiping God, community, and mission. As image bearers we express our identity in Christ through worship to God, community with one another, and mission to the world around us.

The purpose of describing the life of a disciple is to make sure we have a clear picture of what we are trying to accomplish as the church. There are so many causes competing for our resources that having this picture has kept us at Mars Hill Church focused on making disciples. Here is a brief summary of the aspects of a disciple's life and how they apply to community:

IMAGE OF GOD (*IMAGO DEI*)

We are image bearers of God, created in his image to proclaim his greatness to the rest of creation. This is who we are, not what we do. This means that we have intrinsic value as his image bearers and that we were created for a purpose—to acknowledge the glory of our Creator.[5] It is from the image of God and the reconciling work of Jesus on the cross[6] that we express our identity as disciples of Christ through worship to God, community with the body of Christ, and mission to the world.

IDENTITY

Our identity is in Christ. This means that we define ourselves in the same way that God does: by what Jesus has done on the cross.[7] We are not defined by what we have done or by what we do or by the things that we have. Jesus has atoned for our sin,[8] clothed us in righteousness,[9] and adopted us as sons and daughters.[10] This is our identity. As a community, this means that Jesus is our King and Savior. He is our highest affinity, the Bible is our highest authority, and the Trinity is our example for how we live together in community.

WORSHIP

We are worshipers. We are created as instruments of worship intended to behold the glory of God and praise the name of Jesus.[11] Therefore, our greatest joy comes when we do what we were created for: worship Jesus. We worship through song, gratitude, prayer, and the way we live our lives.[12] As a community, this means that we worship together and encourage one another to "proclaim the excellencies" of Jesus.[13] Our life together is a proclamation of the gospel of Jesus Christ and a corporate act of worship.

COMMUNITY

We are the body of Christ created in the image of God, who exists in community.[14] The Father, Son, and Holy Spirit have eternally existed in relationship with one another as one God in three persons.[15] God is a relational being who created us as relational beings so that we could image him.[16] As a community, this means that we are to reflect the goodness of God and preach the gospel through our lives together. This means loving one another, forgiving one another as Christ forgave us, calling one another to confession and repentance for the purpose of reconciliation, and challenging one another to lives that glorify God.[17]

MISSION

We are missionaries created in the image of a sent and sending God. God sent his Son, Jesus, into human history to reconcile himself to us.[18] God is in the business of gathering more worshipers to himself. As his disciples, our mission is to proclaim the gospel of Jesus so that more image bearers would come to a saving faith and worship God.[19] As a community, we are called to live lives together that reflect God's goodness, mercy, and grace, showing the world around us the saving and transforming love and power of Jesus Christ.

Therefore, we are called to live our lives intentionally and missionally, not only loving our brothers and sisters, but also engaging with and loving our neighbors. We do this because we are commanded to,[20] and so that hopefully our neighbors will see the glory of God being lived out in our lives, stirring their hearts to answer God's call for their own salvation.[21]

By keeping our eyes on the vision of being disciples in community, we remain focused on Jesus, following him and enjoying the fruit of being his disciples. If, however, our leadership is reactionary, we risk making disciples that are underdeveloped in some areas of discipleship. This happens when the need we are addressing only requires one or two of the three expressions of our identity. For example, when we focus on care and Bible study, we develop disciples who don't know how to apply their knowledge to reaching the lost and sharing with others the love they have for one another. In contrast, we want to be a people who, being reconciled to Jesus and one another, exhibit all three expressions out of our identity in Christ.

WHO WE ARE VS. WHAT WE DO

In taking the time to describe the life of a disciple, we must be careful not to build our identity on doing these things, but rather understand these expressions as who we are. We have been conditioned to find our identity in what we do. However, Scripture tells us that we are children of God adopted through the grace of Christ, through whom we derive our identity. My identity is not what I do; I do *out* of my identity. Worship, community, and mission come out of who I am as a disciple of Jesus. This then is a response to what Jesus has done for us. It is in receiving his grace that we get to *be* disciples.

That being said, if this is our picture of a disciple, it is also our picture of a healthy community. A community group is just the aggregate of its members. If a group is missional, it is because the members of that group are missional. If a group is not, this is indicative of a deficiency in the participants of that group. In this way, community groups are great barometers of how well the church understands the gospel. If they have been transformed by the gospel, then it will show in the community life of the group.

With this in mind, let's take another look, as we did in chapter 1, at the great picture of community in 1 Peter 2. In context, Peter is describing how we as believers ought to conduct our lives in light of what Christ has done on our behalf.

> But you are a chosen race, a royal priesthood, a holy nation, a people for his own possession, that you may proclaim the excellencies of him who called you out of darkness into his marvelous light. Once you were not a people, but now you are God's people; once you had not received mercy, but now you have received mercy.
>
> Beloved, I urge you as sojourners and exiles to abstain from the passions of the flesh, which wage war against your soul. Keep your conduct among the Gentiles honorable, so that when they speak against you as evildoers, they may see your good deeds and glorify God on the day of visitation.[22]

Just as we did with our description of a disciple, Peter begins with our identity. He gives us four ways to understand whom we are rooted in, who Jesus is, and what he has done. We are a "chosen race," reminding us that we have been set apart and are predestined to follow him.[23] We are a "royal priesthood," reminding us that through the death and resurrection of Jesus, we no longer need a mediator between God and us.[24] We are a "holy nation" through the imputed righteousness of Jesus, and we are a people of God's "own possession."[25]

Everything we are called to be comes out of what God has already done. What a beautiful picture of God's love. We have been born again through the resurrection of Christ. We are new creations that are no longer slaves to sin but slaves to righteousness.[26] God is jealous and unwilling to share possession of his people with sin. I always picture my kids when I read this verse. I love kids in general, but I have a passionate love for *my* kids. That's how I see this rolling off of Peter's pen. We are God's kids!

All four aspects of our identity are rooted in Jesus and, significant to our topic, are plural in nature. These are corporate identities of a race, priesthood, nation, and people. As the church, we need to recapture our sense of community and connectedness to one another. Peter reminds us that we are indeed a people, not a collection of individuals. Community groups are a people who understand their identity in Christ and have a corporate or communal understanding of that identity. This means that we are committed to one another and to our collective growth in Christ.

Then, out of that identity, we worship; we "proclaim the excellencies" of Christ.[27] Through Jesus we have been reconciled to God and to one another. Once we were not a people, but now we are God's people through the mercy of the cross.[28] Therefore we ought to be a people who point to and worship Jesus consistently. If the group you call your community does not regularly point you to Jesus and remind you of his grace and mercy in your life, then it is not a gospel-centered community group. We are a people in awe of what Jesus has done and we worship him accordingly.

Out of that worship, Peter challenges us, in verses 11–12, to live lives that reflect the transformation that comes from the gospel penetrating our lives. Because we have been made a holy nation, we can live holy lives. Often at this point in the passage we begin to read from a personal rather than corporate viewpoint. We are accustomed to understanding sanctification in an individualistic manner. However, the context has been plural, written to the church, and remains so as Peter calls us to fight against our flesh. Because Christ has reconciled us and made us a people of his own possession, the church is oriented toward one another's corporate sanctification.

Emphasizing this point, Peter calls our fight against sin a "war." Now, contrary to any Rambo movies you may have seen, wars are not fought by individuals. Armies fight wars. John Piper has made the point that the church has been deceived into believing that we are in a time of peace while our enemy stays on the assault.[29] Our deception has lulled us into being unprepared and ill equipped for battle, leaving many of our number maimed or killed by ambushes of sin. Within our community groups we must remember that we are in a war against sin and that we fight together for the truth of who God is and what he has done.

Finally, out of our identity we understand the purpose of having a good reputation, as a community, with unbelievers.[30] We maintain a good reputation not so that we can judge the lost or so that we might think highly of ourselves but so that the unbelieving might come to believe. Even if they malign our characters or slander our names, we must desire that they come to know God. We are called to be a community that is on mission with God. It is important to note that Peter describes a community whose good deeds are seen by nonbelievers. We must be a community that is seen loving one another and our neighbors. Don't miss this point. If no one ever catches us being Christians because we are holed up behind drawn curtains, then we are not a missional community.

So we see in this description of a Christian community that our corporate identity is in Jesus, and out of that comes worship, community, and mission, culminating in the glorification of God. This is our picture of a healthy community group. In sum, the purpose of community is to make and mature disciples of Jesus; everything else is the product of that purpose.

LIFESTYLE VS. EVENT

Key to being this type of community is to redefine community groups as a lifestyle rather than an event. When we see community as a series of events, we hold on to our individuality and see community in terms of what it offers us. If we are to live in community in the way that Peter describes, then we need rethink our lifestyle.

Peter's picture of community is one in which people consider one another, prefer one another, and sacrifice for one another. This will require a paradigm shift from the thinking that one's walk with Jesus is solely personal. It requires us to see ourselves as a people and not just a gathering of people.

The irony in our tendency to shrink from such a notion is that we were made for community, as we discussed in chapter 1. This means that when we experience this kind of community, it will fill the many holes we feel are disconnecting us from one another. If we pursue God because we have been reconciled to him through the cross, then why would we not pursue one another? We have been reconciled to each other through that same cross. We cannot call ourselves a community if we continue to compartmentalize our lives.

I am not advocating building a commune but rather consciously considering one another and including one another in the everyday moments of life. This can be done by simply inviting members of your community into the rhythms of your life that you typically do by yourself. If your family goes out for pancakes on Saturday morning, why not invite another family to join you? Maybe invite a newly-wed couple from your group so they can experience the chaos of dining out with small kids. This is a simple act that may even seem mundane, but the blessing that comes from sharing your life with others is invaluable, and it is the difference between autonomy and community.

One of our leaders recently committed to making his group a life-style rather than an event. The group met as usual on Tuesday nights for dinner, prayer, and Bible study. To mix things up, though, he made a standing reservation at a local restaurant for Friday nights. It was a completely optional time to hang out. The group, being accustomed to typical small group events, didn't take to the idea right away. Yet despite some thin turnouts, the leader stayed committed to the extra time together. Eventually members of the group started trickling in to the restaurant on Fridays. It transformed their group.

It seems surprising that such a simple gesture would be that significant, but the change was dramatic. They went from being a Bible study to being a community. They began to meet before Sunday services so they could worship together as a community. They began to prefer spending time together. Suddenly they were excited to invite nonbelievers to their group because it was a source of life. The most amazing thing was that they saw four of these new folks come to know and worship Jesus in a span of three months. When they began to live in community as a lifestyle, it began to give them life, and they wanted to share that experience with others. The gospel became real and tangible, and those around them saw it and gave glory to God.

LIFE GIVING VS. LIFE TAKING

This brings us to another essential characteristic of gospel-centered community groups and the goal of this book. Since community is a blessing of God, a community group should be life giving to its members. Unfortunately, many of our experiences have been different. Community groups are often seen as obligatory and life taking. We secretly hope the kids will be sick so we can stay home. We know if we go, then Sally is going to dominate the conversation with the same issues that we've heard for the last three weeks, and insensitive Rob is going to miss the point and start lobbing verses at her. As this drags on, Jim is going to try to prove he is the smartest guy in the room by parsing a Greek verb and quoting dead Puritans. Then, just when time is running out, we will go through prayer requests for each other's aunts' cats that are suffering from angina. My only prayer will be that it ends soon so I can go get one more piece of banana bread and get home to my TV. This is not a picture of community. Yet many of us have settled for this experience because we don't know better or because we consider it a modern form of self-mortification.

So let me give you permission to avoid the "circle of awkwardness." When we get together over a meal, why do we fill it with idle chatter about the local sports team and *American Idol* and then transition to "spiritual" time in a drum circle? What if we reclaimed the dinner table for meaningful conversations about what Jesus has done and how the Holy Spirit is leading us today? We don't have to be in a circle to talk about conviction, repentance, and the excellencies of Christ. When we relegate these conversations to specific times of "care and share" or Bible study, we are effectively compartmentalizing our lives. We are propagating the belief that these conversations and convictions should not spill over into unsanctioned times. We condition people to make a mental separation between spiritual and practical matters. When should our talk not be salted with the gospel? I am not saying that every conversation has to be an exegesis on propitiation. There are times for small talk and banter about our favorite sports teams. But if we talk about Jesus only during Bible study, if we pray only in that circle, if we cannot articulate the gospel's influence on our view of politics, business, sports, and entertainment, then we are not living transformed lives. We are still compartmentalizing the gospel.

That is if we truly understand the gospel. Let's not miss the most glaring problem. If groups are not giving life, the cause may be as simple as people not knowing how to speak life and truth to one another. In order for our groups to be life giving, we must understand the power of the gospel and believe it. I have made the mistake of assuming that the people of my church really understand the depth of what Jesus did on the cross and how that affects every aspect of our lives. This is why we preach the gospel every Sunday. We have no need for a new message because the gospel never gets old. But preaching it every Sunday does not guarantee saturation. Developing life-giving groups requires equipping them to apply the truths of the gospel to the trials, hopes, joys, and relationships of life.[31] As they learn to speak life, they will begin to experience life. Think of the gospel as the water that makes life grow. No gospel, no life.

I have run into so many people who have stopped participating in community groups because they were life taking. What a tragedy! This is not what God intended for his church. Community is a life-giving blessing from God. John Piper, speaking of church membership and the participation of the church, put it this way, "[Community] is a blood-bought gift of God's grace. More than most of us realize, it is a life-sustaining, faith-strengthening, joy-preserving means of God's mercy to us. I urge you not to cut yourself off from this blessing."[32]

Therefore, if our community groups are not life giving, we must ask why. If community is naturally life giving, then we must be doing something to thwart it. Take the time to understand why, and take permission to rethink your group so that it becomes a place that is life sustaining, faith strengthening, and joy preserving.

CREATIVITY VS. CONFORMITY

So what do we actually do in a community group? Now that we have established that we are defined by who we are in Christ and not what we do, I am ready to discuss this topic. In Acts 2:42–47, we see a picture of the church living life in community. This gives us a nice picture from which to build our expectations for what community groups can look like:

And they devoted themselves to the apostles' teaching and the fellowship, to the breaking of bread and the prayers. And awe came upon every soul, and many wonders and signs were being done through the apostles. And all who believed were together and had all things in common. And they were selling their possessions and belongings and distributing the proceeds to all, as any had need. And day by day, attending the temple together and breaking bread in their homes, they received their food with glad and generous hearts, praising God and having favor with all the people. And the Lord added to their number day by day those who were being saved.

What we see in this text is a list of things (that I will call elements of community) that marked the early church: study, fellowship, communion, spiritual gifts, care, generosity, mission, prayer, and worship. What we do not know is exactly *how* they did these things. We do not have a prescriptive picture of what this must look like, and in that we have freedom. Groups are unique expressions of the gospel lived out in community rather than cookie-cutter copies. Consider the elements discussed below to be like paints. We all use the same paint to produce a picture, but each painting will be a unique work of art. The way these elements are employed and experienced by a community group will be unique to the people, culture, context, language, and neighborhood. The goal is to see unique expressions of community that encompass these elements within the rhythms of the group rather than dictating a one-size-fits-all experience.

Though we may not study the Bible every time we get together, we are committed to its study and authority in our group. We may worship together on Sundays, pray on Tuesdays, and fellowship together on Thursdays. In other words, don't expect that every element of community will be expressed every time we gather, but that each element has its place in the rhythm of our group. Experiment with different rhythms and elements to develop community groups that are life giving and transformational. Below are some elements of community that can be incorporated into the rhythms of any community group.

BIBLE STUDY

The church in Acts dedicated themselves to the apostles' teaching.[33] A key element in our community groups is the study of Scripture. The Bible is the revelation of God and is authoritative in our lives. It is a gift of God's grace and is our opportunity to know him; therefore, the study of Scripture is a consistent rhythm of any group. At Mars Hill we prefer to see our groups follow the sermon series. This connects the proclamation of the Word on Sunday with the lives of our people during the week, producing the transformation cycle we discussed in chapter 2. As I've said before, this does not mean that Bible study is the primary purpose of groups. Rather, Bible study is one element used toward the purpose of making and maturing disciples of Christ.

CONFESSION AND REPENTANCE

The communities in Acts celebrated communion with one another on a regular basis.[34] Implied by this rhythm is their culture of confession and repentance. The purpose of studying Scripture is to know God and how the good news changes everything. This transforms our lives as we respond to the gospel.

Because Jesus has atoned for our sin and removed its stain, we want our community groups to be marked by a culture of repentance. This is a response to the gospel and the work of the Holy Spirit. Because our identity is defined by Jesus, we don't have to fear death or shame.[35] We can be open and honest about our struggles as we put sin to death[36] and confident in the compassion and grace of our Lord as it is expressed through our community. To see transformation in our community groups, we need to constantly remember what Jesus has already accomplished on our behalf and remind one another of that daily. Again, we are a holy nation, a people of his own possession;[37] therefore, as a community we cannot wink at sin but must lovingly correct beliefs, thoughts, and behaviors that are not honoring to God.

The purpose in reflecting God's patience and grace must always be reconciliation, not conformity. Reconciliation is the gospel. Conformity is religion. Therefore, the goal of a group is to point to

Jesus, the cross, and the resurrection as the only remedy for sin and to look to the Holy Spirit for the ability to walk in righteousness. We want heart change through the power of the gospel and not merely behavioral change. This requires that our community groups be saturated with the gospel to the place where it spills into every area of our lives. Don't assume that your community is there. If they don't understand the gospel, then they will never get to confession and repentance.[38]

WORSHIP

The early church was continuously praising God in worship. As the image bearers of God in community, we must live lives of worship. The purpose of confession and repentance is to align our hearts with God so that we can rightly worship him. We confess and repent of idols to which we have given worship that only Jesus deserves. Worship of Jesus is the destination for confession and repentance and is a natural outflow of a community group. As a community we are to encourage one another toward constant worship, pointing to the works and glory of Jesus. This can take on many forms, from singing songs to enjoying a steak dinner, but it is a consistent part of any community group in response to the wonder of our God.

PRAYER

In addition, the early church was dedicated to prayer.[39] Prayer is a gift of God's grace to us—we have the opportunity to communicate with our Creator. We have the ability to converse with God, praising him, confessing our sin, asking for his provision, and listening for his response. When a couple is struggling with infertility, we get to seek God for peace and patience. When a friend gets a job offer, we get to praise God for his provision. When a family miscarries, we get to mourn with them and ask God for comfort. We cannot expect to be Spirit dependent if we are not committed to prayer as a community. Our community groups must be consistently seasoned with prayer. Within the rhythms of a community group, prayer can be spontaneous as the need arises, or it can be ordered and a regular expectation of meetings. Regardless of how it manifests, prayer is an integral part of any community group as it reflects our dependence on our Father. If we are to be a people who walk in the Spirit, we must be quick to fall on our knees before the Father.

HOSPITALITY

We see the early church eating together and enjoying one another in fellowship.[40] This is the place where you can more easily invite new people to experience your community. Gospel-centered hospitality seeks to love people where they are while providing a safe place to introduce someone new to your group. Hospitality includes both the way we prefer one another and the way we open our doors to those who need to meet Jesus. The early church took care of one another and welcomed outsiders. Hospitality is our privilege and joy as ambassadors for the gospel.[41]

EXERCISE OF SPIRITUAL GIFTS

The Holy Spirit is in the business of exalting Jesus, and that is the purpose of our community groups.[42] The community in Acts saw many manifestations of the Holy Spirit within their midst. Therefore, it stands to reason that we should be exercising our gifts in community and seeing the fruits of the Spirit used to edify the church. As the church is described as a body with all the parts important to its function, so as a community of believers we have the privilege of exercising our gifts for the sake of Jesus's name. When discerning the appropriateness of particular gifts in community, remember that the purpose of those gifts is to exalt Jesus.

MISSION

The last thing we see as a product of this community in Acts 2 is that God added to their number.[43] Mission is an essential element of any group as we engage with our neighborhood for the fame of Jesus and the advancement of the kingdom of God. As we receive the kingdom through the cross and resurrection, we get to share it with the lost. This is the outward focus of your group, to love people and share the truth of the gospel through the witness of your lives together. This is the consistent focus of any community, in both prayer and action. We will dig further into what this looks like in the following chapters.

BLESSING VS. OBLIGATION

As we have been exploring the idea of redefining community, I hope I have given you a vision of what community groups can be. We have been reconciled through the blood of Jesus to be a community that exalts him. As we work from that vision, we can be a community that allows the gospel to saturate our lives and fulfill our purpose to make disciples and worship Jesus. Community groups that are steeped in the gospel will grow in their understanding of who they are in Jesus and will be more inspired to proclaim his excellencies and share the good news.

This picture of community is not a pipe dream. This is the experience God intended for us to have in community. He created us for it and made it possible by sending his Son to die on the cross. Through the resurrection of Jesus we are a community. We just need to be it. When our experience doesn't match up, it is not time to throw in the towel but an opportunity for us to call one another back to this vision. I know that building relationships within a community group can often feel obligatory. I think that is why Scripture often depicts the process of sanctification in terms of a battle. It is going to be work to glorify God in community. But when we understand community as an expression of our identity in Christ, we open the door for living out our faith in community in ways that give us life. We will begin to see ourselves as a people called to exalt our Father in heaven as disciples of Christ. In doing so we redefine what a community group is, aligning our definition with what God intended for us, namely, to reflect his glory through community as we make disciples of Jesus.

5

NEIGHBORHOOD

A NEW APPROACH TO MISSION

In the last chapter we set our goal to develop community groups that honor God and exalt Christ. We want to be a community of people who submit to and worship Jesus through prayer, devotion to Scripture, and praise. We want to be groups who are joyfully obligated to one another for the sanctification of the church, while fully committed to the mission of going and making disciples for the glory of Christ because we have been reconciled through the cross. This can be summarized as community that images God through worship, community, and mission. While most people expect expressions of community and worship within a community group, the expression of mission is generally a pain point for most small group ministries. Mission is generally the most neglected aspect of community within the church today. As we discussed in chapter 3, ownership of the mission is often abdicated to the church as an institution or to designated "missionaries." I want to challenge our perceived limitations in regard to mission in community and show you how your group can get their boots on the ground in the mission of God.

Much has been written over the last decade on the idea of *incarnational ministry*. God entered into history to redeem us from our rebellion, and therefore we should, as his ambassadors, bring the gospel into culture rather than detach from it. *Incarnate* means to embody, typify, or represent. We are called to embody the gospel within the world.

In John 17, Jesus tells us that he is sending us into the world even though we are not of this world. We have been given to Jesus by the Father, and now we get to proclaim his goodness to the world. This concept is anchored in our purpose to image God, and I am therefore all for incarnational ministry.

The question is: What does incarnational church look like? The conversation on this subject has produced a variety of churches with diverse interpretations of what it means to be incarnational. I am convinced that it is more than edgy music and candles. Incarnational ministry will begin with the mobilization of the saints to embody the gospel in community. Jesus broke into our world, lived among us, and changed everything. That just makes Christian coffee shops seem trite. You cannot build a ministry that requires the world to come to it and call it incarnational. We have to go. We have to go into the world as ambassadors of Jesus.

This conviction has inspired the vision for community groups within Mars Hill Church to mobilize the body for the advancement of the kingdom of God—to see the name of Jesus exalted in our city and yours through the proclamation of the Word and the incarnation of the gospel through community. Around this conviction we have built a missional strategy for reaching our city by building our groups around particular neighborhoods that have distinct cultures and people groups. Community groups are structured geographically around these neighborhoods and focus specific missional efforts on reaching these neighborhoods. We call this the neighborhood approach.

VIRAL EXPANSION OF THE GOSPEL

The goal of the neighborhood approach can be summed up by the idea of saturating the city with the gospel of Jesus Christ. Community groups have the ability to fill every nook and cranny of our city as outposts of the gospel.

In urban planning, one of the goals is to build urban density. As you concentrate people and businesses within a small area, you produce efficiencies in development and maintenance while driving more commerce. The goal is to reduce urban sprawl, or the spreading out of the city into more suburban areas, which results in more roads and utilities to maintain. Basically, the goal is to concentrate people in the urban core.

The goal of ministry is to increase the gospel density of our cities, to concentrate the gospel where the people are. We need to saturate the city so that it cannot help but be blessed by the church as it lives out the gospel within it. When we see the church as a people within the city, we can see the potential for spreading the gospel everywhere the church is, rather than just gathering once a week at a particular location. Groups on mission give us the ability to see the gospel infect and affect the whole city.

As gospel density increases with the growth of groups, these groups can begin to collaborate together to reach whole neighborhoods and regions of the city. As groups draw more people to Jesus, they replicate and increase the gospel density of their neighborhoods, increasing the likelihood that more of their neighbors will be positively impacted by the gospel. In this way we can strategically advance the gospel and see whole cities transformed by the death and resurrection of Jesus.

CONTEXTUALIZATION

The effectiveness of this strategy (or any missional strategy for that matter) will be determined in part by the church's ability to contextualize the gospel. Contextualization is the communication of the gospel in a particular place, time, and culture, to a particular people, in a way that it can be understood without diluting its truth.[1] The church has been commissioned to proclaim the gospel to the ends of the earth, reaching all tribes and tongues. This makes contextualization of the gospel crucial to the success of the church.

Therefore, we need to think about how we do this in our own context. One of the mistakes I see in the church today is that although we understand the need for contextualization, we often use the wrong tool for the job. More accurately, we try to use one tool to do every job.

If, however, we understand the tools we have at our disposal, then we can be more effective.

For instance, our church services can contextualize at a macro level, but community groups can contextualize at a more specific level within a neighborhood. Furthermore, individuals can contextualize at the level of personal experience. There are some overlaps as well. A community group can contextualize at both the neighborhood and personal level while a church service's depth of contextualization may depend on its size. A small church, for example, may speak very specifically to a particular neighborhood or people group. What is important, however, is that we recognize the opportunities and limitations of each expression of the church. When we do, we can appreciate the capacity for community groups to sharpen the point of the gospel message within our context. For large churches, especially multicampus churches like Mars Hill, this becomes increasingly critical. At Mars Hill I see four levels of contextualization:

1. MARS HILL: GENERATIONAL CONTEXTUALIZATION

The proclamation of the gospel from the pulpit of Mars Hill transcends any particular place and really speaks to a generation of the unchurched and dechurched of our culture. This is what I am calling generational contextualization. People around the world listen to Mark Driscoll's sermons, which still communicate the gospel in a way that is effective across many contexts. In addition to Driscoll, there are several preachers around the country and world who speak to our generation, such as John Piper, Matt Chandler, Tim Keller, and others. Obviously, not every church will have the platform to speak to this level, but depending on the size of the church, it may be contextualizing to a region or a city. Smaller churches will start by contextualizing at the local level.

2. CAMPUS: LOCAL CONTEXTUALIZATION

At Mars Hill, the campuses are the vehicles for contextualizing at the local level. Campuses oversee an area of a city or a particular city within a region. Each campus has a particular context of culture and people groups to whom they need to articulate the gospel. These variables result in different programs, aesthetics, forms of communication, and even music.

3. COMMUNITY GROUP: NEIGHBORHOOD CONTEXTUALIZATION

Campuses, however, cover many different people groups and cultures. Today, our largest campus, situated in the Ballard neighborhood of Seattle, actually covers nine distinct neighborhoods of north Seattle, from the independent and bohemian Fremont to the more family-oriented Greenwood neighborhood. Because they live and play there, our community groups can contextualize the gospel in these neighborhoods in ways the campus as a whole cannot. They know the neighbors, their needs, and their language. Groups can be designed to reach their neighbors and may look different from neighborhood to neighborhood.

4. DISCIPLE: PERSONAL CONTEXTUALIZATION

Lastly, each person in a neighborhood is unique and has unique experiences. Each member of the church has an opportunity to articulate the gospel to someone and contextualize it to his or her personal experience. Because groups are organized to inspire ownership, members are ready and willing to share the gospel when an opportunity arises.

Spaces Diagram

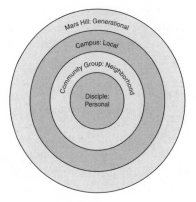

As I said before, the size of your church and the context that you are in will determine your focus and scope for the articulation of the gospel. By recognizing the particular strengths of different aspects of the church, we can more effectively reach our cities for the gospel and advance the kingdom of God.

TRANSIENCE

Such contextualization at the community level requires a commitment to a particular neighborhood; therefore, we need to talk a bit about one of the bigger difficulties with developing long-lasting, intentional community today. The transient lifestyle of our culture makes geographic community increasingly difficult, especially in urban areas. Peter Block, in his book *Community: The Structure of Belonging*, describes our society today as fragmented and in need of transformation:

> The need to create a structure of belonging grows out of the isolated nature of our lives, our institutions, and our communities. The absence of belonging is so widespread that we might say we are living in an age of isolation, imitating the lament from early in the last century, when life was referred to as the age of anxiety. Ironically, we talk today of how small our world has become, with the shrinking effect of globalization, instant sharing of information, quick technology, workplaces that operate around the globe. Yet these do not necessarily create a sense of belonging. They provide connection, diverse information, an infinite range of opinion. But all this does not create the connection from which we can become grounded and experience the sense of safety that arises from a place where we are emotionally, spiritually, and psychologically a member.[2]

Block recognizes that we, as a society, are becoming increasingly disconnected and in need of transformation. We have become a nomadic people who pick up our lives to follow the next best opportunity. We move to find more affordable housing, better jobs, or just a change of scenery. There is little that anchors us to our homes anymore. For Block, the answer is a more connected society with a sense of belonging. But what provides that connection? What unifies scattered, disconnected lives?

Growing up, I lived in the same house for eighteen years. During that time, my parents never changed jobs. In contrast, my wife and I moved four times in the first four years of marriage. In the first ten years after graduating from college, I made three *career* changes, let alone job changes. Stability seems to be an idea from the past.

Contributing to this instability is the reality that the business world in our generation is marked more by efficiency than by loyalty. Companies hire and fire as the market for their product goes up and down, and employees jump from company to company to get the biggest paycheck. I will leave it to the experts to determine which came first, but what we can say is that this self-focused approach to employment has made setting down roots increasingly rare.

Thus, when we cast a vision for establishing the church in the neighborhoods of our cities, we must contend with the transience of our culture. We have two options. The first option is to seek to understand how our transient culture organizes and align our methods to match it. If people organize by affinity or life stage, then we build groups around these affinities to best reach them. In other words, we adapt to the transience of our cities by building the culture within the church to match.

The merit in such a strategy comes down to relevance. The purpose of adaptation has to be contextualization of the gospel. This means that we adapt so that we can help people understand the gospel better. If, on the other hand, the motive for contextualization becomes fitting in, we have wasted our time at best and have lost the gospel at worst. So, if you are going to build gospel-saturated community in a way that is palatable to moving peoples, it must proclaim the truth of the gospel. The problem is that we are called to be a people with a corporate identity, as we discussed in chapter 1. Loose relationships, void of obligation to a corporate holiness, are antithetical to the gospel.

The root of our transient culture is individualism, but the world is in tension between belonging and autonomy. People want to belong to something, but only for what they get out of it. They want to belong without an obligation to anyone. Decisions are primarily made based on what benefit it has for me as an individual. Community just doesn't work that way, and conforming to such a culture is precarious.

There are times and situations in which adapting aspects of community to the culture does not compromise the gospel. In these cases we can use the way we organize community to reach more people for the gospel. Organizing community groups by affinity or life stage can have merit, and we will discuss this later. After all, this is how people naturally clump into tribes. But my concern is that when we use this as our primary factor for organization, we reinforce a consumer culture and dilute the gospel truth that we have been reconciled to one another through Jesus.

As fallen people, we want a group to meet our needs and keep us from getting uncomfortable. Jesus, however, brought together fishermen, tax collectors, prostitutes, and Pharisees. He challenged them to look beyond the external and their own comfort. He drew people together who had to be reconciled through his blood in order for them to share a meal together. To make this possible today, we have to see community as more than a place to meet our own needs. Calling people to that kind of community is calling them to a great blessing. One of the coolest experiences in a community of believers is seeing the eclectic mix of people God has drawn to himself through Jesus to accomplish his mission. So affinity-based groups have their place, but building groups around the mission of God will create opportunities for the gospel that affinity groups cannot.

The second option is to offer people an alternative. The reasons for a transient society are rooted in individualism and have been exacerbated by the volatility in the work force. Consequently, our society, which has grown up on a steady diet of individualism, has nothing to anchor people to a particular place and time. People don't take the time to get to know one another, and they have no corporate identity. So when a better house or job becomes available, there is nothing to miss when they leave. First Peter says that before Jesus we "were not a people."[3] This is what I see when I look at our neighborhoods today. People don't talk to each other. One can live on the same block for ten years and never share a meal with someone across the street.

Sadly, the church has not been immune to this loss of community. Robert Putnam, in his book *Bowling Alone*, points out that "Americans' involvement in the social life of the church beyond worship itself—in Sunday schools, Bible study groups, 'church socials,' and the like—appears to have fallen at least as fast as church membership and attendance at worship services"—at least by one-half since the 1950s.[4] Putnam summarizes this statistical decline:

> In sum, over the last three to four decades Americans have become about 10 percent less likely to claim church membership, while our actual attendance and involvement in religious activities [like community groups] has fallen by roughly 25 to 50 percent. Virtually all the postwar boom in religious participation—and perhaps more—has been erased.[5]

Putnam goes on to point out that as our generation has grown up in a disconnected culture, it has imported that culture into the church.

> The decline in religious participation, like many of the changes in political and community involvement, is attributable largely to generational differences. . . . The slow but inexorable replacement of one generation by the next has gradually but inevitably lowered our national involvement in religious activities.[6]

In other words, a detached generation has created a culture of community within the church that reflects the uncommitted, nomadic characteristics of the culture outside the church. How tragic is that? The church is supposed to be an oasis from the destruction of sin in the world. Because it is made of a people created in the image of God who exists in community, the church should be a place where the cultural longing to belong and to be known is satisfied, not echoed.

So do we accept this attribute of our culture, or do we provide an alternative? Is it possible that if we had personal connections within our neighborhoods, if we belonged to a people, that we would become less transient? The church living out its faith in community with a love for Jesus and a love for its neighbors can provide an antidote for a transient society. It can give people a reason to stay in the neighborhood. It can provide an anchor that transcends the next reason to move.

People have a desire to belong. Block's "essential challenge is to transform the isolation and self-interest within our communities into connectedness and caring for the whole."[7] He recognizes the need to be connected and belong, even if he does not acknowledge that this need is derived from our identity as image bearers. When we transform neighborhoods, we tap into that basic desire. The church has an opportunity to provide an alternative to a nomadic culture, and, by doing so can connect with a longing in the hearts of disconnected people.

The gospel should have the effect of taking individuals who were not a people and making them God's people. We can provide an alternative to the patterns of the world. In so doing, we give our neighbors an opportunity to see how the blood of Christ has affected our lives in a way that is more compelling than telling them. They get to see it. What they will see will not be perfect lives but lives that are filtered through the gospel.

Interestingly, in cities such as Portland and Seattle that sit atop the list for unchurched cities in America, the neighborhood revolution is already beginning. Participation in neighborhood centers is on the rise, and neighborhood identity is in vogue. There are no fewer than twenty-nine separate neighborhood blogs within the city limits of Seattle. In a cultural shift of global economy and unlimited information, people such as Block and Putnam are recognizing the need to localize while we are globalizing. There is a sense that we are more insignificant today because of the pace of information, and people are looking to belong to something local and tangible. We can already see our culture's desire for belonging. Ironically, Block finds the solution for belonging in a familiar place for us. He writes:

> The future is created one room at a time, one gathering at a time.
> Each gathering needs to become an example of the future we want

to create. This means the small group is where transformation takes place. Large-scale transformation occurs when enough small group shifts lead to the larger change. Small groups have the most leverage when they meet as part of a larger gathering. At these moments, citizens experience the intimacy of the small circle and are simultaneously aware that they are part of a larger whole that shares their concerns.[8]

Block believes that the way to change a disconnected and fragmented culture is by people gathering in small groups who care for one another and live life together. Interesting. If the world sees the need for society to be transformed in this way, I want the church to be at the front line of that fight. I want the church to be the vehicle for that transformation. The gospel is the remedy that the world is longing for and the only remedy that can truly transform.

VETTING THE NEIGHBORHOOD APPROACH

With this in mind, I want to challenge you to a missional strategy built on community groups reaching their neighborhoods. There are four questions that must inform any missional model for community groups:

1. Is it accessible?
2. Does it inspire ownership?
3. Is it effective?
4. Is it scalable?

Let's discuss how the neighborhood approach responds to these four questions.

ACCESSIBILITY

Two years into our marriage, my wife and I purchased our first house. It was during the height of the Seattle housing boom, when the average time a house stayed on the market was four days. That's not a typo. We are talking pan-seared tuna. These things hit the market and were snatched up. So when a "for sale" sign sprang up in one of the neighborhoods we were watching, we jumped on it. To show

how quickly we jumped, the lock box hadn't been installed yet but we found a key in the mailbox and checked it out. Before the house was actually shown, we had an offer in. This wasn't a great house but it had potential—which is a nice way of saying that it needed a ton of work. Once purchased, it was time to see how rough the old diamond was. It turned out to be Clint Eastwood rough. This thing was going to be a testament to physical redemption.

Three weeks later, the glow of our purchase was wearing down. I began to estimate the remodel. During this process, I discovered that the basement floor I intended to finish had a fondness for seeping water. This was not good. As I contemplated everything required to fix the house and make it livable, I was overwhelmed. I would have to remove the basement slab, dig it out, drain it, and pour a new one. I would need to redo the plumbing, electrical, and exterior of the house, not to mention new framing, windows, chimney, furnace, hot water heater, and much more. Adding to my dismay was the reality that I had never done any remodel work before. I was overwhelmed to the point of paralysis. The vision was so big that I had no idea where to begin. As I sat in the damp basement, crowbar in hand, I could not see how I was going to redeem this house.

So it is with the mission of the church. It takes vision to lead the church, and our God is a big-vision kind of God. Think about Abraham becoming a nation, the exodus, building the temple, and building the church to the ends of the earth. God is into big visions. So the answer is not to suppress the vision of the church. Leaders should dream big. But we need to make the mission of the church accessible to the church itself.

When I broke down the vision for my house into manageable tasks, I was able to move again. I could focus on the smaller task of rewiring without worrying about the plumbing. That would come later. This gave me little victories to look forward to as I completed the latest step toward the greater goal, which inspired me on to the next.

This is the goal of the neighborhood approach. We want to make the mission of the church accessible to the members of the church so that they are not paralyzed by the vision but instead are inspired toward ownership and participation. By taking the greater mission of the church and breaking it down into smaller missions for each neighborhood, we make the mission accessible to anyone. This is bite-sized mission.

As a member of the church, it can be difficult to understand how I could meaningfully serve my city and make a difference. It is much easier to see how I could serve my neighbors and make an immediate impact on their lives. That is something I can get my hands around. After all, average members don't have a website or a blog or a microphone. However, if you were to ask them to permeate the gospel on their blocks by loving and serving their neighbors, they could get ahold of that and be excited. When all members of the body of Christ use their gifts to contribute to the mission, they are able to accomplish the big-picture mission. The strategy of reaching our cities by focusing groups on neighborhoods makes this mission accessible to individual members of a community group and helps them see how they are participating in advancing the kingdom of God.

OWNERSHIP

In chapter 3, we discussed the necessity of ownership when it comes to the mission of the church. So when it comes to organizing community within the church, we need to build it to inspire ownership. I am sure you have heard the old adage, "Give a man a fish and he eats for a day; teach a man to fish and he eats for a lifetime." When building a ministry, we generally consider a goal that we are trying to accomplish and then organize and build systems to achieve this goal. When we do this in such a way that the ministry delivers fish to our people, we inspire conformity rather than ownership. We condition people to accept the fish we give them and expect them to come back next week and ask for more fish.

We do this by building systems that don't require missional participation from the members of the church. When they can sit back while the church staff does all the work for them, from outreach events to assimilation, they have no reason to learn to fish.

We don't want to hand people fish, we want to hand them fishing poles. Jesus gave Peter a picture of disciples as fishers of men.[9] In looking at some classic models of small groups, you would be left with an odd view of a fisherman. You would assume that a fisherman sits in a small boat with other fishermen and picks up a fish once a week at the grocery store and takes it back to the boat. This isn't fishing. If we want to have missional churches that reach people for Jesus through our community groups, we need to build them in such a way that each leader is taught how to fish.

The neighborhood approach inspires ownership by giving leaders responsibility. It gives them something to own. It teaches leaders to lead by giving them something big enough that they need to rely on the Holy Spirit to be successful. By leading a neighborhood group, leaders need to pray through a vision for their neighborhoods group, build a plan for achieving it, and inspire the members of their groups to carry it out. The more we can share that responsibility with leaders, the more they will own the mission. The more leaders own the mission, the greater the impact we will have for the gospel as a church. And as we discussed in chapter 1, raising the expectations for leaders will be met with higher levels of leadership.

When it comes to ownership, the goal of the neighborhood approach is to inspire every community group leader, every community group coach, and every community group pastor to see themselves as missionaries to the people in their cities. We spend a great deal of time and energy preparing overseas missionaries to understand the cultures and peoples to whom they are going to minister. Missionaries learn new languages and customs as they prepare to live in new countries. We train church planters to be anthropologists, studying the cultures of their cities. We want them to understand their context so they can present the gospel in a way that is compelling to the people of that city. We do the same for new campuses, tailoring each to reach particular people groups and demographics.

Rarely, however, have I heard of churches taking the time to teach their members to be students of the culture. For some reason, when it comes to community groups, we often settle for stamping out community in a box. Pastors take the role of missiologist for the city but don't invite their leaders to study the culture with them. Either that or we copy a program that has had success somewhere else and expect it to work in our context as well. Certainly these mistakes happen at the church planting level, but it is almost guaranteed at the community group level.

While flying back from a conference on the East Coast, I picked up a book by Ed Stetzer and David Putnam called *Breaking the Missional Code*.[10] It is a book for church planters to help them understand what it means for a church to be truly missional and how missional churches have broken the code in reaching a culture that couldn't care less about the gospel. While reading it I was inspired to share it with my leaders and coaches. You see, if I understood how to decipher my city, then I could tell my leaders how to reach it. But if I could teach my leaders how to interpret their neighborhoods, then they could devise many more ideas to reach the city than I could ever imagine. They could become fishermen.

When leaders become anthropologists of their neighborhoods, then we begin to see unique expressions of community that are designed to reach a distinct person, place, and time. The possibilities are endless, and ideas aren't bottlenecked by one mind. Rather than community in a box, we have a kaleidoscope of expressions that can reach people who would never darken the door of a church. Teach your leaders to be missiologists, and you will have taught them how to eat for a lifetime.

EFFECTIVENESS

Is it effective? I am surprised at how many people never ask this question about the ministries they lead. We are often satisfied with ministries that meet needs but are ineffective for the mission to which God has commissioned us. Jesus has called us to go and make disciples, so when we ask if our groups are effective, essentially we are asking if they are making disciples. If our community groups are not making disciples, we are wasting our time.

In chapter 4 we discussed what we are trying to produce in a disciple: a believer who finds his or her identity in Jesus and expresses it through worshiping God, loving one another, and being missional to the world. This means that effectiveness can be seen in saints who are growing in their faith and devotion to Jesus and also in the conversion of nonbelievers. If both of these things are happening, then our groups are successful.

The neighborhood approach is effective because it connects people who have the gospel to people in need of the gospel. Jesus painted the vision of the church being *in* the world but not *of* the world.[11] He was talking about his disciples, the body of Christ, you and me, being the connection of the church to the world. By focusing community groups on a particular neighborhood, we can build personal relationships that bridge barriers to the gospel in ways that we cannot through a church service alone.

This not only makes new disciples, but it also addresses the need to mature disciples within the church. It has become commonplace for church members to see their participation in the mission of God as merely inviting people to a Sunday service or giving money to overseas missions. Although we should do these things, these activities never require Christians to employ the gospel themselves. I have seen many churches where it would be possible for members of the church never to feel compelled to articulate the gospel to another human. This is tragic for those people's neighbors and friends who need to hear the gospel. It is also tragic for them. They will never experience the joy of God using them as an instrument of transformation. They won't witness new life as the Holy Spirit regenerates someone before their eyes. It is a gift from God that they never open.

The Great Commission is not an obligation. The Great Commission is a life-giving, life-changing gift of God. By calling Christians in our churches to participate in proclaiming the gospel, we are developing them as disciple-making disciples. Driscoll has said many times that Mars Hill Church exists for those who are not here yet. This mindset is vitally important for the continued growth and health of the church. We need to continue to shepherd people to have an outward orientation toward advancing the kingdom of God. In doing so, we are shepherding them toward maturity and developing them as healthy disciples of Jesus. In this way, the neighborhood approach is effective for making and maturing disciples of Christ.

SCALABILITY

The last question I want to ask is whether such a strategy is scalable. Building a structure that has to change if and when it is successful doesn't make a lot of sense. Therefore, we want to build a structure that can not only grow but also handle significant growth. When building community groups at Mars Hill, this was a significant design criterion. We wanted a robust but nimble structure—two concepts that don't usually work well together. However, by encouraging ownership and decision making at the edges, we were able to accomplish a pretty good compromise between the two.

As we will discuss in chapter 8 on the structure of groups, we work with a common cascading structure of pastors, head coaches, coaches, and leaders. When we began restructuring our groups, we had one pastor, four coaches, and about twenty leaders. At the time, Mars Hill was already a regional draw, with people traveling all over the Puget Sound to attend on Sundays. We didn't, however, have much density. People and groups were spread out. So when we started, each coach oversaw a region of the Puget Sound, some of which included multiple towns. Groups were connected to their coaches and drew people from around a local region. As we grew and replicated groups, these original regions became the campuses we have today. Those campuses have broken down the mission into neighborhoods, as we have been discussing.

As gospel density increases, the groups provide a core for launching new campuses with little to no change in the community group structure. This is achievable because the structure is able to grow with the church. Let's take a quick moment to do some math. Here is the data:

A group leader oversees up to fifteen people.
A coach can oversee up to six leaders.
A head coach can oversee up to six coaches.
A pastor can oversee up to six head coaches.

In this structure, one pastor can reasonably oversee up to three thousand people. (Although, at that size of a congregation, your head coaches will probably be pastors, as well.) What makes this approach scalable is that by developing even one head coach, you increase your capacity to shepherd thirty-six more groups. Thirty-six groups consist of over four hundred people! This is significantly more people than attend the majority of churches in America, at less than one hundred people each.[12] A well-trained coach can shepherd around ninety people with a span-of-care (which we will discuss more in chapter 8) less than one to six. That is pretty amazing.

This speaks to why it is so important to develop coaches, as they can multiply your ministry effort. But what is startling is the fact that you can shepherd so many people by just adding one coach or one head coach. The effect is multiplicative rather than additive.

An added but significant bonus is that this structure, in conjunction with the neighborhood approach, provides ample opportunities for leadership at various levels and capacities. A common problem in the church today is that there are often very few opportunities for young leaders to strive for. Either there simply are too few spots to lead from or the only opportunities presented require a significant amount of training before they can be filled.

Harkening back to the advice that Jethro gave Moses: some leaders have the capacity to oversee tens, others hundreds, and others thousands.[13] The neighborhood approach values leaders at every level and gives young leaders the opportunity to rise to the level of their calling. There is a place for everyone to exercise his or her gifts for the advancement of the gospel.

DEFINING NEIGHBORHOODS

As we vetted the neighborhood approach, we saw how it is accessible, inspires ownership, and is effective for making disciples. As well, it is a strategy that helps us advance the kingdom of God in a way that is able to grow when God blesses it. The last thing I want to address is the question of how you define neighborhoods. The purpose of defining neighborhoods is to help define an attainable mission field to which a community of God could minister. Because churches are different sizes and have different contexts, we need some latitude in how we define neighborhoods. Here are some things to consider:

1. SIZE MATTERS

The size of your church and the size of your context will determine how you define a neighborhood. If you are a church with ten community groups in a city with ten neighborhoods, it will not be advantageous to break down your groups by literal neighborhoods. One of the goals of this strategy is to have groups work together to advance the mission. Ten groups targeting ten different neighborhoods will result in a lot of people feeling like they are on an island. A better plan would be to define a "neighborhood" as a region of the city. In this way, you can rally groups around a local mission and develop gospel density. As that occurs, you can localize your definition of neighborhood. At some Mars Hill campuses that span a large region, the neighborhoods are defined as towns that the campus draws from. As the campus grows, they will begin to redefine those neighborhoods to better serve and reach those towns and possibly plant campuses in each. The goal is to grow to the place where your defined boundaries are the same as the self-recognized boundaries within your city (not necessarily the municipal boundaries). In this way, you align the mission of those groups with the self-identifying characteristics of the people to whom they are trying to contextualize the gospel.

2. AFFINITY

Many churches organize groups by affinity or life stage. The benefit of such groupings is that people are usually more comfortable in a house of mirrors. This makes these groups much easier to fill, as they attract like-minded people. One of the downsides is that they lose the blessing of diverse perspectives that comes from groups who have multigenerational/ethnic/gender/socioeconomic backgrounds. The second downside is the inability to galvanize these groups toward mission. Being made up of similar people from different parts of a city may make it easy for them to get along with each other, but it makes it difficult to share life together if those lives don't overlap at the grocery store. The exception is when the affinity is around a particular people group who actually inspires mission. For example, a group that wants to reach the snowboarding community builds a community group of snowboarders. This is a great reason to build a group by affinity. If you want to do this well, make sure that every affinity group has a defined mission, a plan to make the group missional rather than a Christian club, and a way to stay on mission. These groups can be very effective at reaching marginalized people groups within the city. Affinity groups can organize around music cultures, sports cultures, ethnic cultures, and more. As long as they are motivated by mission rather than comfort, they can be very effective.

3. MIX IT UP

There is nothing that says that you can only do either geography-based groups or affinity-based groups. Having both options available is perfectly acceptable if that will help your church advance the gospel more effectively. While affinity-based groups are often very attractive, I have found it to be presumptuous to assume everyone has a people with whom they identify. As helpful as a targeted group is to its target, it also excludes those who don't identify with it. Most people will have an easier time identifying mission with their neighborhood that they drive through daily rather than with any particular people group. That is why I have found that organizing groups around geography as our primary structure and allowing affinity groups for people with a passion for a particular people group to be the most effective.

4. DON'T MIX IT TOO MUCH

Give people options and they will opt. If you build a structure with too many options, you will have a harder time casting a clear vision and being effective for the gospel. Build your groups with a primary focus and allow for exception when it is best for the kingdom. Otherwise you dilute your call to mission and confuse your leaders. It also becomes a nightmare to manage. Geographic groups make it simple to know who is responsible for shepherding whom. Groups organized by relationships break down when there are no preformed relationships. Every option outside of the neighborhood structure will require additional oversight and administration, so choose the options you offer carefully.

EMPOWERED TO MISSION

As you can see, the neighborhood approach is an important tool for advancing the kingdom of God in our cities. It allows the church to mobilize its members to the mission that God has for us, to advance his kingdom. By breaking down the mission into attainable pieces, we are able to saturate the city with the gospel and to let loose a viral expansion of the kingdom. This allows us to contextualize the gospel at various levels within our city and provides an alternative to the transient culture of our generation. At Mars Hill Church, the neighborhood approach is an integral part of our community group ministry. As we have seen, it has answered the questions of accessibility, inspiration of ownership, effectiveness, and scalability. By empowering our people to own the mission through the neighborhood approach, we have the ability to change our cities in ways the church has failed to do for generations. Because we are all in Christ, we can all proclaim the good news. May your city never recover.

6

SPACES

ENGAGING CULTURE

Now that we have established the benefits of a neighborhood approach, it is time to turn our attention to how the mission of God plays out in those neighborhoods. The need for such engagement and the possibilities for evangelism should be clear by now. Hopefully you have already been thinking about what that might look like for your community groups. I imagine that thinking about engaging your neighborhood has caused some tension in your mind regarding what a group looks like and what a group does. The assumed definitions of a community group or a small group generally do not have a category for engagement. The idea of engagement is inherently offensive. If your groups are passive (or worse, defensive), this transformation will require a significant paradigm shift. We need to think differently about what it means to be in community together. We need to think differently about what it means to be a missional church.

As I have said earlier, community groups have a great deal of potential for advancing the gospel and seeing people come to know Jesus. But to see this type of transformation, groups need to be active in the mission of God. The good news is that when believers are equipped, they have all the motivation they need in Jesus. The challenge is that churches and pastors have gotten in the habit of doing what God has called his *disciples* to do. In this chapter we want to begin equipping the saints, his disciples, for ministry by first giving them some new categories for what it means to be in community and on mission.

BARRIERS AND BRIDGES

It makes sense for us to first acknowledge that there is resistance to the gospel. Whether you live in Seattle or in the Bible Belt, there is resistance to the transforming work of the gospel. In some places there is an overt rejection of Jesus and of the reality of God. In other places the resistance is more covert. The assumption of the gospel and the smuggling of religion into Christianity is its own form of resistance. The former resists the truth and law, while the latter resists grace and sanctification.

To move from passivity to activity for the gospel, we need to repent of our apathy, commit to the missional work of the gospel, and learn how to engage. Assuming that we have dealt sufficiently with the first two steps in previous chapters, we will focus here on the third. As we do, I want to give you a word of caution. As we talk of engaging culture, it is very easy to objectify what *culture* means. The use of generalization and ideologies causes us to drift from seeing culture in terms of people. Our focus moves from wanting to see people saved by grace to seeing ideas crushed by truth. When we dehumanize culture, we start to be agents of condemnation and death rather than heralds of good news. So as we discuss common resistances to the gospel, fight for compassion for the blind and deaf. Remember that we are talking about people who cannot see and cannot hear and need the grace of God to open their eyes and ears.

Daniel Sanchez, in his lectures on the importance of story in expressing the gospel, talks about identifying barriers to the gospel and building bridges to overcome these obstacles.[1] Here are my definitions of *bridges* and *barriers*.

> *Barriers*: Issues of *practice*, *culture*, or *perception* that inhibit the progress of the gospel.
> *Bridges*: Opportunities for people to encounter the truth of the gospel through conversations and experiences with the people of God.

Our goal is to remove any unnecessary barriers to the gospel so that the only stumbling block for people is Christ crucified, as Paul says in 1 Corinthians. Unfortunately, today the church itself often presents more of a barrier than Jesus. As the bumper sticker says, "I like Jesus; it's Christians I can't stand." The idea behind barriers and bridges is honest self-assessment and a willingness to adapt, as Paul says, to be *"all things to all people,* that by all means I might save some."[2] Let's look at the particular examples of barriers.

Practice: Barriers of practice are the practical obstacles of time, space, and accessibility that hinder the gospel. A large meeting at the church building can seem cold and impersonal. If this is the only opportunity for someone to hear the gospel, then the space itself can be a barrier. In the same way, a community group meeting in someone's home can be considered extremely intimate and intimidating to someone new. We have to ask ourselves if there is anything about the space or times of our gatherings that presents a hurdle to our neighbors belonging to our communities.

Culture: Cultural barriers include language and behaviors that alienate people before they can hear or experience the gospel. Language is a common, and tricky, example. In some contexts, the use of "colorful" language is seen, even from the perspective of a nonbeliever, as disrespectful and inappropriate. In these cases, the use of such language is socially unacceptable and will build a barrier to the truth that you want to share. In other contexts, however, if such language offends you, you would be considered judgmental and religious, again forming an obstacle to the gospel. By understanding the cultural barriers to the gospel in our contexts, we can prevent building new barriers, begin to address existing barriers, and instead build bridges to Jesus.

Perception: Barriers of perception are the images, stereotypes, or experiences that people have had with the church that affect their perception of Jesus and the church. For instance, if a church has a reputation of being separatists, then they are not going to help the cause of the gospel by starting a food bank in the church when a secular food bank exists down the street. Partnering with organizations that have a common goal will begin to redefine the perception of the church within that neighborhood. In Seattle, our participation in park and street cleanups with municipal organizations has provided many opportunities and built several bridges within the city.

As we identify barriers to the gospel, we can begin to build bridges to our neighbors. Bridges will look different in every context, but they start with a community of believers who have been changed by Jesus and want to share that joy with the world around them. A bridge is anything that provides an opportunity to your neighbors to be blessed and to experience the grace of God through your community.

BECOMING A MISSIOLOGIST

Identifying barriers is the beginning of becoming a missiologist. To be a missiologist is to be observant, having your eyes open to the values of people in your city and particularly in your neighborhood. It is about discovering where people find their identity, what wakes them up in the morning, where they spend their time, and where they hope to experience community.

As we begin to assess the barriers in our neighborhoods, we have three categories for engaging with the world. At Mars Hill we talk about receiving, rejecting, and redeeming culture.[3] Engagement with culture should be active rather than passive. Engagement is an action. We want to observe culture and filter it through the Word of God to determine our response to it. As we approach any cultural offering, we may receive it, reject it, or redeem it.

Receive: We can accept many aspects of culture that are not in opposition to the truth of Scripture. If the Bible does not explicitly or implicitly prohibit a particular behavior, value, or experience, and it can be accepted without opposing our consciences, then we are free to accept it. This simply means we can participate in it without modification and enjoy it to the glory of God.

Reject: There are some aspects of culture that are naturally opposed to the gospel. Slavery and abortion are obvious examples, while self-actualization and self-atonement are subtler but no less dangerous. These are concepts that we need to reject and provide an alternative to through the gospel.

Redeem: Some aspects of culture may be inherently innocuous, but they have been perverted by sin. These are things that were made good by God but have been used for idolatry or abuse. Sexuality would be a good example. Sex is a gift from God that he intended to be enjoyed between a husband and a wife. Sadly, the world has perverted sexuality. We don't reject it because it has been perverted, and we don't accept it as it is presented by the world. Instead, we redeem it and call one another to experience it in the way that God has intended.

SPACES

Now that we are starting to think differently about the opportunities to engage with our neighbors that we have through community groups, we need to expand the reach of influence of our groups. That influence is going to come through engaging with our neighbors as we share experiences and conversations with them. This truth is supported by secular research as well:

> John McKnight has studied communities for 30 years and found that community is built most powerfully by what he calls "association of life," referring to the myriad ways citizens come together to do good work and serve the public interest. Whether in clubs, associations, informal gatherings, special events, or just on the street or at breakfast, neighborly contact constitutes an uncounted and unnoticed glue and connection that makes good communities work.[4]

Block and McKnight are saying that transformational community happens when we live life together. If this is true, then we cannot expect the gospel to have an impact on our neighbors by osmosis. They are not going to spontaneously experience the love of Jesus through drawn curtains. If we are going to have a gospel impact in our neighborhoods, we are going to have to engage in life with people on our streets.

In his book *The Search to Belong*, Joseph Myers explores the changes in our generation with regard to belonging.[5] He borrows a concept from Edward Hall's book *The Hidden Dimension*.[6] In his work on anthropology and social behaviors, Hall identifies "fields" of interaction that influence the perception and behaviors of people and determine the acceptable level of intimacy. Myers uses these distances to identify multiple spheres of belonging as we walk through life. Each distance or space has its own purpose and ability to influence us in life. Hall sees them in the way we make culture and develop as people, while Myers sees them in terms of the way in which we belong to each other.

Hall's/Myers's Spaces:
Public—12 feet +
Social—4 to 12 feet
Personal—18 inches to 4 feet
Intimate—0 to 18 inches

When we understand these spaces and distances, we begin to understand why traditional small groups have a hard time engaging culture. If we only offer interaction in the personal and intimate spaces in the form of Bible study and prayer, we should not be surprised when people find such interaction to be too high of an energy barrier to overcome. If we want to have an impact on culture, we must find a way to engage it at various levels of intimacy.

BELONGING BEFORE BELIEF

One of the observations that Myers makes in his book that is particularly important to our discussion is the idea of belonging before belief. Essentially, he argues that, unlike previous generations, people today are willing to participate in a community even if they do not yet share the beliefs of that community. Even more important is the understanding that people will become functioning members of a community, such as a church or a community group, before they commit to believing in the community's values. They want to see if such communities are authentic, and they are willing to take a test drive.

Jim has been coming to Mars Hill for almost a year now. He

wandered in to a Sunday service for reasons he can't really explain, but since then he has been a regular fixture on Sunday mornings, sometimes being present at multiple services. Most Sundays I find him in the lobby reading books, which he finishes and puts back in the bookstore.

Did I mention that Jim likes to talk? I have had many conversations about the gospel with Jim, as have most of the staff and various members of the church. These conversations have been fruitful, but Jim is still not sure he is willing to accept the implications of God existing and dying for his sins, though it has brought him to tears many times.

But here is the curious thing: Even though Jim has not submitted his life to Jesus, he is an active member of a community group and serves on the soundboard on Sunday mornings. Even more amazing is the fact that Jim has brought multiple nonbelieving friends to church services and to talk to me or other pastors. To summarize, Jim is in community, serving, and evangelizing, but he is not a believer! At this point, he is a healthier member than the majority of Christians that attend churches each week. This example may be a bit extreme, but it lends credence to the idea that people are willing to get close enough to see if what they hear of the gospel is real. They long for it to be true because they have been failed by so many false gospels before.

This should be a game changer when it comes to community groups. If this is true, then one major barrier for someone joining your group has been dismantled. It is, however, a double-edged sword. Our groups must live the gospel to be effective, but what an opportunity! In light of this observation, we must be more committed than ever to engage our neighbors and provide them space to get close to lives that have been transformed by the gospel.

In his book, Meyers makes great observations of our culture and asks great questions of the church. I do not, however, think that Meyers makes the right conclusion at the end of the day. While I think his work has merit for its observations and questions, it fails to make a compelling argument for the ultimate goal of belonging. Belonging is not enough. We need to belong to Jesus. Our goal as disciples of

Jesus is to call people to a saving relationship with Jesus and to belong to his church. This implies a tension. We need to be accepting of sinners in need of grace, as Jesus was, without being satisfied with belonging that does not lead to belief and life transformation.

SPACES OF ENGAGEMENT

In light of our goal to call people into a deeper relationship with Jesus, I have modified the spaces concept and applied it to how community groups can engage with their neighborhoods. These spaces are how we belong to one another *and* how we engage with the culture around us. Roughly applying Myers's concept of spaces and belonging from intimate to public and filtering them through a grid of engagement, I have come up with four basic spaces in which community groups can exist within their neighborhoods: fellowship, hospitality, service, and participation.

Spaces Diagram: Intimacy

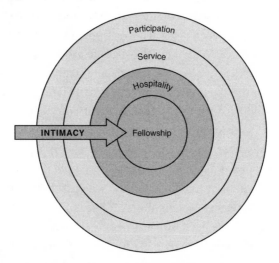

Fellowship: Times to encourage one another in our lives with Jesus.
Hospitality: A safe place for anyone to belong to our communities.
Service: Meeting the practical needs of our neighborhoods.
Participation: Participation with our neighbors in common spaces and events.

We can see these spaces in the description of the church in Acts 2:42–47:

> And they devoted themselves to the apostles' teaching and the fellowship, to breaking of bread and the prayers. And awe came upon every soul, and many wonders and signs were being done through the apostles. And all who believed were together and had all things in common. And they were selling their possessions and belongings and distributing the proceeds to all, as any had need. And day by day, attending the temple together and breaking bread in their homes, they received their food with glad and generous hearts, praising God and having favor with all the people. And the Lord added to their number day by day those who were being saved.

Although we should acknowledge that the picture of community in Acts 2 is descriptive rather than prescriptive, we do see in this description of the first-century church an expression of community that aligns with the expectations found in Scripture. Our community groups do not need to look exactly like the first-century church (especially the church at Corinth), but we should use what we know of the church, and the convictions that inspired it, to influence how we do community today.

We see the space of *fellowship* in their devotion to the teaching of the apostles, prayer, worship, confession, and repentance. We see the space of *hospitality* as they broke bread, had favor with all the people, shared food and possessions, and many people were added to their community. By distributing food and possessions to those in need, we see that they *served* the practical needs of those around them. Further, their reputation among the people indicates that they served them and *participated* in life with them.

Engaging with our neighbors across a variety of spaces opens doors for having a transformational effect on culture as a whole. Again, Block writes,

> The context that restores community is one of possibility, generosity, and gifts, rather than one of problem solving, fear, and retribution. A new context acknowledges that we have all the capacity,

expertise, and resources that an alternative future requires. Communities are human systems given form by conversations that build relatedness. The conversations that build relatedness most often occur through associational life, where citizens show up by choice, and rarely in the context of system life, where citizens show up out of obligation. The small group is the unit of transformation and the container for the experience of belonging.[7]

Thus, Block recognizes the need for engagement and the power of small groups to effect change. Granted, community groups are only a vehicle for the real power of transformation solely found in the death and resurrection of Christ. But Block does recognize how passionate people united by a clear vision and mission can effect change in our culture. Therefore, having a community that engages with culture across these various levels of intimacy can help the church spread the gospel and advance the kingdom of God, just as it did for the early church.

COME AND GO

Before we break down each of these spaces, you will notice in the diagram that the spaces of fellowship and hospitality are a different shade from the spaces of service and participation. This is because there is a fundamental difference between these spaces. These spaces break down into "inward" ministries (fellowship and hospitality) and "outward" ministries (service and participation).

Inward ministries are those ministries that require someone to come to you. In one sense, they are passive. Like the mantra from *Field of Dreams*: "If you build it, they will come." As we break down these spaces, you will notice that they require people to make the effort to participate. This does not mean that they are bad, just that they have a relatively high energy barrier.

Outward ministries, on the other hand, require the group to go. These spaces are active. They require the group to get involved outside of their living rooms. If you are going to win a championship, you need to learn to win on the road. Consider these spaces the testing ground for being a good road team.

In Acts 5, we learn that the early church was known for meeting at Solomon's Portico. This was a public location within Jerusalem where they gathered to teach and live life together. They met in homes as well, but they didn't hide there. They lived where they would be seen. As the church, they lived in multiple spaces, public and personal.

In doing this, they set an example for us of what it means to be sent by a sent and sending God. Jesus commands us to go. He wants us to be active and seen. As we consider what it means to live in multiple spaces in community, we need to find a balance of both inward and outward ministry.

FELLOWSHIP

With that in mind, let's break down each of these spaces as they pertain to our community groups. The most common place for a community group to find itself is in the space I am calling fellowship. This is the space for Bible study, prayer, confession, and repentance. This is where most small groups spend the majority of their time together, and it is an essential space for community within the church. Acts 2:42 tells us that the early church "devoted themselves to the apostles' teaching and the fellowship, to the breaking of bread and the prayers." The study of the Bible and prayer are hallmarks of the church living in community with one another. As we discuss other spaces, we need to remember that our community groups should be devoted foundationally to Scripture, prayer, worship, confession, and repentance.

Because we discussed these elements in chapters 4 and 5, we don't need to go into detail here. As a matter of fact, most groups are comfortable with these expectations. The challenge is to build a community where these are natural and authentic. We know we should be a community marked by confession and repentance, but we don't always know what that looks like. Even a devotion to Scripture can have the life sucked out of it if we don't approach the Scriptures as a life-giving source of living water. As we discussed in chapter 5, the space of fellowship is about building a natural, authentic community that loves Jesus and his Word and pursues one another with gospel intentionality. Hopefully by now you have a picture of what that can look like and a desire to fight for that experience in your community groups.

A common mistake in the church today, as we put more emphasis on contextualization and mission, is to neglect the fellowship aspects of community. We have some expectation that this happens on the level of the individual, but we ignore the communal nature of these elements of the Christian life. At the end of the day, we are a community of believers. We follow and worship Jesus as our Lord and Savior. If we connect with our culture and neighbors but don't bring them into a fellowship of worship of Jesus, then we have missed the point of the church.

Additionally, we need to be aware of where people are spiritually when they join us in this space. Having a nonbeliever join my group does not prevent me from leading our group in times of prayer and confession. What it *does* do is require me to explain and teach the group about what we are doing. This will not only be helpful for the guest, but will be valuable for the entire group. Don't assume that because someone has gone to your church for a while that they know how to pray or what repentance looks like. Having a guest or new member join your group can be a great time to explore the group's understanding of these elements.

With that said, when we *only* exist in the fellowship space, we have a problem. When we do this we form what Driscoll calls "holy ghettos." No one but the most religious would dare to venture into such spaces. People will take the long way to avoid *that* block. Taking a wrong turn and finding themselves in such a group, nonbelievers slowly lock the car doors and pray—maybe for the first time—that they will get out alive, never to return. We must understand that fellowship is the most intimate of spaces and is therefore the most intimidating place for a new relationship to be built.

When we live only in this space, we become isolated. The church lives in the tension between syncretism and separatism, as Driscoll articulates in chapter 6 of *The Radical Reformission*.[8] Understanding this tension is not just important in the way we articulate our values, but in how we practically live our lives as well. The lack of emphasis on the Bible, prayer, and other aspects of fellowship in community leaves us in danger of becoming "of the world," while exclusively living in this space keeps us from being "in the world" to proclaim the gospel of Jesus.

Keys:
Be Christ centered and devoted to Scripture.
Be intentional and authentic.
Be grace filled and truth telling.
Avoid the "holy ghetto."

HOSPITALITY

Hospitality is the first step to being a missional community group. Most forms of hospitality will still be on your turf, making it a "come" ministry, but it shows gospel intentionality to invite people to belong to your community. Developing hospitality is as easy as throwing a party. Christians really need to repent of their inability to party. Jesus announced himself by performing his first miracle at a wedding party and was accused of being a drunkard and sinner because, presumably, he wasn't afraid to enjoy himself in the company of sinners. He didn't sin while having a good time, nor should we. But he was not afraid to mix it up. We should repent and throw some parties and invite our neighbors.

Parties are not, however, the only event in the space of hospitality. Any time we provide the opportunity for someone to belong in our community group before belief, we are operating in this space. That might be a standing reservation at your favorite restaurant, a bowling league, a pick-up football game on a Saturday morning, a poker night, a knitting club, or any other regular event to which you can invite someone new.

As you think about how you can lead your group to exist in the space of hospitality, consider some factors. First, the purpose of hospitality is to welcome people into the group by lowering the energy barrier for them to feel as though they belong. This means we have to be thoughtful of the experience they might be having. Christians are notorious for not being self-aware. We get so entrenched in Christian culture that we don't realize that what feels normal to us may be very intimidating for someone else.

Homes are a good example. I worked for the same company for almost eight years, and I rarely recall having dinner at a coworker's home, let alone being invited to the home of their friend whom I had never met. In Seattle's culture, this would not be considered odd. Going to a stranger's home is intimidating. Therefore, it could help to find a neutral third place if we want someone to feel comfortable. Being missional begins with thinking of the preferences of the people who aren't in your community rather than your own preferences. This can affect the food you serve at a party to the music you play. As a group, you need to be oriented toward your guests rather than to each other.

The worst thing you can do is throw a party and invite the neighbors but ignore and alienate them when they show up. Consider their experience and invite them to belong, just as they are, and just as Jesus did with you. As those relationships grow, you will eventually have an opportunity to invite them into deeper fellowship. If you truly care about people, then it will be a natural invitation. If they feel as though they belong and are accepted by your group, then they may be willing to risk the intimacy of joining your group to learn about Jesus.

Taking these concepts into account, my community group gathers regularly at a local restaurant as part of our natural rhythm of community. We have a standing reservation every other Thursday night. It is just a natural part of our life together. It is a time to connect with the group, and it provides a neutral, welcoming place to introduce someone new to the group. Some folks' only connection to our group is Thursday night happy hour. They aren't ready to join us for our fellowship gathering, but they do get to see how the gospel shapes our lives through these social events. They are still looking in to see if what we say of the power of the gospel is real. As they become more comfortable with us and see the transforming power of the gospel in our lives, they will eventually stick their toes in the water. And when they do, they will have confidence that they already belong to our community and that it is a safe place to wrestle with the claims of

Jesus. It really is that easy. It doesn't take any preparation to eat dinner and enjoy one another, and in a society that is dying to belong to something, it is an easy invitation.

Keys:
> Be self-aware.
> Lower the energy barrier to belong.
> Meet people where they are.
> Offer a welcoming experience.

SERVICE

So far we have stuck primarily to the inward ministries that are safely within the boundaries of our own turf. Some of the spaces where we venture are neutral territory but are still an invitation into our comfort zone. Most groups live their lives between the fellowship and hospitality spaces. But as we established earlier, if we are going to be a missional church, then we need to get off the couch, move out of the circle, and go. Tying in our convictions from chapter 1—that God uses people to advance his kingdom and that we are created in the image of a sent and sending God—we need to be an active community. Peter said people would see our good works, and that would cause them to glorify God.[9] This implies that we are doing good works. It also implies that we are doing good works that are noticed by our neighbors and bring glory to God rather than ourselves. In Jeremiah, God called his people to seek the welfare of the city.[10] Even in exile they were to live out their faith in the promises of God. He wanted to bless them and those around them in order to display his glory. We, too, ought to seek the welfare of our cities.

That is what the space of service is all about. It is blessing the city in practical ways. This requires you to understand your neighborhood and know what needs exist that you can meet. Very few of us have any clue about what is going on in our neighborhoods and where we could easily serve them. Ironically, the needs are endless. As I write this, I recently talked with a local organization that serves the elderly in the city, and they had 180 senior citizens on a waiting list to get help around their homes or going with to the grocery store. And those are just the ones that signed up for help. In Seattle there is an entire municipal department dedicated to finding help for local neighborhood projects like park maintenance and street clean-ups. Service projects can range from volunteering as a group to help during a local festival to cleaning up the yards of the elderly in your neighborhood. It might look like helping a neighbor move or planting trees in the median on your street, but the point is to bless the city because Jesus has blessed us.

So how do you find out what the needs in your neighborhood are? You can start by asking. Get to know your neighbors, talk to grocery store clerks, and become members of your neighborhood association—and actually attend the meetings. Our groups have had great success just showing up at their local community centers and building relationships with the directors. If you want to see the needs, they are not hard to find. And as you get your group involved in serving your neighborhood, you will begin to find common ground with your neighbors. That is the beauty of serving at the local level. Not only are your neighbors served, but also you can find common purposes to serve together.

Take Jim for example. Jim likes cars. He leads a community group at Mars Hill that draws a lot of gearheads. Part of their service and hospitality space involves fixing up cars. They do *pro bono* mechanical work for low-income families and single moms. Regardless of whether people have met Jesus, it is easy to get them excited about using their talents to help single moms. In this case, the service aspect of the group provides a great opportunity for nonbelievers to be a part of the community while serving and building relationships on both fronts. The act of serving is in itself a testimony to the love and sacrifice of Jesus. It's a bonus that we can have a great time doing it. Whenever we can combine our personal passions with the gospel and our communities, the more sustainable those communities will be.

Keys:
> Meet practical needs.
> Find common purposes.
> Use local organizations.
> Combine passions.

PARTICIPATION

The last space that I want community groups to spend time in is what I call participation. This corresponds with what Myers and Hall call public space. This is when we simply participate in neighborhood activities and events as a community group. Fairly easy to do, but as you know, the church has a bit of a reputation of being a recluse, like an albino tiger rarely seen in the wild. This isolation assaults the gospel in two ways.

First, it ignores the command of Jesus to go and make disciples. This isn't an assault simply because it is a failure to obey. The *desire* to go and make disciples is rooted in the internalization that Jesus is worthy to be worshiped. Mission is about seeing the glory of Christ and wanting to make it known. When we withdraw from the culture, we are saying that Jesus isn't a big enough deal for our neighbors to reckon with.

On the other hand, if we say that we see his glory but are afraid to influence the world, then we assault the gospel in another way. A response of fear ignores the power of the gospel to redeem and communicates a lack of faith in the promises of Jesus. In Matthew 28, after Jesus commands us to go, he promises that he will be with us always, "to the end of the age."[11] As I said earlier, the church must be seen.

So go to block parties, the chili-paloozas, and fireworks displays. Go to the county fair even if the rides are lame. The space of participation is about being a part of your neighborhood. It is about building a reputation of caring for people and for the city. It is about meeting people on common ground and not always expecting people to meet you on your turf.

One of the reasons that we have a hard time inviting nonbelievers into community is because we don't know any. As you start to live in the space of participation, you will begin to develop relationships with people who eat dinner thirty yards from your table whom you have never met before.

Participation can take on many forms, but here are some things to consider. Join events rather than starting your own whenever possible. Church coffee shops can be a blessing to a community, but becoming regulars at a locally owned coffee shop will be more welcome than competition for latte business. Become a member of the neighborhood association and volunteer as a group to help with local festivals and events. Don't believe the lie that you should be doing "church work" instead. This is the work of the kingdom. When people see your good deeds they will give glory to God.[12]

Another key is to understand that participation is about consistency. Being a regular part of the community gives you and your community group relational capital. That capital opens up opportunities to bridge spaces and invite people into service or hospitality spaces. Participating in one event won't build that type of capital. My kids never say, "Hey, Dad, thanks for coming to that one baseball game; I feel so loved." So make being a part of the neighborhood a priority. That does not mean that every member of your group has to attend every event, but there should be a consistent value of neighborhood participation within your group.

Keys:
> Join rather than create.
> Build relationships.
> Hold participation as a priority.
> Emphasize consistency.

COMMUNITY TETRIS

Now that that we understand each space, our next challenge will be linking them together. It's easy to start providing these spaces within a community group yet still not see fruit. In some cases this is just a matter of time, but often it is because we don't take the time to see how the spaces fit together.

The most significant roadblock for nonbelievers attending your community group is a failure to be invited. Surveys among our church's community groups have found that neighbors who are invited to a group, regardless of which space, are exponentially more apt to attend than those who weren't invited. I say that tongue in cheek, but it is often simply as easy as inviting people. Our community group hosts a neighborhood breakfast once a month. We make crepes and cinnamon rolls and serve coffee. Every month we see people throughout the community come to hang out and to be neighbors. All it took to engage the neighborhood was an invitation.

The picture we have in Acts 2 leaves us with an exciting and convicting statement: "And the Lord added to their number day by day those who were being saved" (v. 47). Remember that the fruit we are praying for is lives transformed by Jesus. We want to see people move from death to life. This probably is not going to happen over a bowl of chili at the community center. But when you link the spaces, you provide bridges for people to become closer to hearing the good news. This gives your group members a natural opportunity to invite people into community. In light of this, remember that a plan inspires confidence. We want community to be natural and organic, but that doesn't mean disorganized. Having a plan can still provide authentic community. My wife and I plan family nights, vacations, birthday parties, and so on. Planning doesn't make them less authentic, but it does make them more effective.

George is a community group leader. His group has become a staple of the neighborhood. They have participated in events and worked on several service projects. Knowing that a block party was planned for next month, the group lined up some service projects with the community center. Now when they attend the block party, they have an opportunity to invite someone they just met into a new space: service. After the service event, the group is going to throw a party in the park to provide a hospitality space for all the volunteers. In one Saturday they will provide multiple spaces to engage their neighborhood and live out the gospel.

As we open our eyes to the opportunities around us, we can begin to identify and dismantle barriers to the gospel. Expanding the spaces in which your groups exist will increase their effectiveness for the gospel. Linking those spaces will make your community groups a kingdom force. This requires a new understanding of community groups as a vehicle for mission and kingdom. It requires us to be the church. It requires us to live a lifestyle of community.

As you begin to pray about how your group can be more effective in reaching your neighborhood, consider what barriers exist and how existing in different spaces can help bridge those barriers. In the next chapter we will look at how that changes the day-to-day rhythms of community.

7

RHYTHMS

NEW WINESKINS

We have all been there. Six o'clock on Tuesday evening, sitting in an awkward circle in the living room, trying to think of something clever but not too revealing to say. Jane starts in with an icebreaker: "If you were a piece of fruit, what fruit would you be?" You can't wait for this to end. Thankfully your group leader turns the group's attention to some question from last Sunday's sermon. "Do you agree with what Pastor Jim said about Jesus?" Crickets. As you try to avoid eye contact, your mind wanders to the work you could be catching up on. When the evening finally ends, you feel a sense of relief and accomplishment that you have carried your cross another week. You are excited that you won't have to do that for another seven days, although you do feel a twinge of guilt that you won't fulfill your promise to the leader that you will invite a friend because, truth be told, you would be embarrassed to bring a nonbeliever into this community.

This is not transformational community. Somewhere along the way we equated this with what it means to be a small group and have adopted these rhythms without any thought. We have passively sucked the joy, life, and sanctification out of community. We can experience more.

By now you have probably picked up on the idea that I am not a huge fan of awkward small groups. Community should be a source of life, as we discussed in chapter 4, and we want to breathe life back into community groups. We have spent some time discussing how understanding the gospel and its implications for community can address heart issues. Having our minds renewed by the Word of God with regard to community is the first step to reviving it in our churches. Now it is time for some new wineskins.

"No one puts new wine into old wineskins. If he does, the new wine will burst the skins and it will be spilled, and the skins will be destroyed."[1] In the same way, if we try to cram the ideas we have talked about in the previous chapters into our traditional view of doing community, then something is going to break. In this chapter we need to break through some of the basic assumptions that define a community group. If we are going to pour the new wine of the gospel lived out in community—expressed in worship to God, community to one another, and mission to the lost—then we need new wineskins.

Rhythms are the wineskin of community. An event once a week cannot contain gospel-centered community on mission with God. If we are going to breathe life into community, we must rethink how we practically live life together.

CULTURE OF OPPORTUNITY

During a recent conference a leader asked me how his group would ever reach the people in their neighborhood when they didn't have enough time each week to address the struggles in their group. This question is excellent. It reveals the common distortion that community should be inward focused and the struggle of a group to look up from their own navels. The picture was becoming clear to this leader. Gospel-centered community would take more than a two-hour event once a week.

This type of community requires a complete rethinking of how we see our participation in a community group. What if your community group was a people rather than an event? When I think of the people I love and enjoy being around, I start to dream of opportunities to be with them. The body of Christ should be like that. This doesn't mean that we don't have events within a community group.

It simply means that we define our group by the people and relationships in it rather than the events themselves.

An event-based community is one that predominantly sees the event once a week as their community group. It defines a community as a time and place. Opportunity-based community is the idea that we are always a community group whether we are together or apart. Each morning I have breakfast with my family, and we read the Bible and pray. Afterward, I kiss my wife and kids and go to work for the next nine hours or so. I come home after work, and we eat dinner and spend the evening together. At what point am I a part of the family and at what point am I not? Being a part of my family is part of my identity and affects the way I live when we are together or apart. I think about them when we are not together, and I can't wait to be with them again. I think about ways to bless them and how I can share my experiences with them throughout my day. That is how a community group with a lifestyle perspective of community functions. When we are part of such a community, we are always on the lookout for opportunities to include one another in common moments of life. If we can create a culture of opportunity, then we can change the way we think about community within the church.

One of the keys to developing opportunity-based community is shepherding your group to be self-organizing. One mistake that leaders often make is that they feel obligated to attend or plan every event. Not only will this fry a leader, but it also makes it difficult for members of the group to develop any sense of ownership. A leader may have to get the ball rolling, but once a group experiences authentic community, it can begin a perpetual rhythm of natural community.

When a community group becomes opportunity based, countless possibilities open up. Everything becomes an opportunity to worship, serve one another, or share the gospel. Taking my family out for pancakes on a Saturday morning becomes an opportunity to invite another family that we want to get to know and encourage. Garage sales become a time for fellowship. When going to the store, we think of one another and pick up an extra gallon of milk. We help build fences and paint houses. We live as a community.

A NEW RHYTHM

Breaking free from an event-focused view of community is not that easy. Most of our small group experiences have been event-based Bible studies or something similar. In order to break such patterns, we must begin by reimagining the basic rhythms of community.

Rhythms can be defined as the when, where, and what of the community. For our discussion we will call them the *time, scene,* and *substance* of a community group. For example, the canonical event-based community group meets at 7:00 p.m. every Tuesday night (when/time), in the leader's living room (where/scene), for a Bible study (what/substance). This becomes the rhythm of the group. On Tuesdays we are a community, and the rest of the week we are living our lives individually.

When these rhythms are rigid and finite, a community group will remain event based. Rigid group rhythms often produce inauthentic and labored groups. Challenging these rhythms is the beginning of reinventing your community group.

I want leaders to constantly ask questions about why they do things. Why do we meet at this time? Why do we meet in this place? Why do we do this when we get together? Does this give life? As we ask these questions and realize that community can be more than once a week, we are on our way to living, breathing community groups.

As we answer these questions, however, the goal is not simply to live life together more. The goal is to be inspired by the death and resurrection of Jesus to live differently. We want to offer more opportunities because we love our brothers and sisters and we have an urgency to share the love of Christ with our neighbors. Don't settle for a new system. If we want to effect change in the lives of our neighbors, we must be willing to be destroyed and rebuilt by the gospel. The questions of time, scene, and substance are questions about how we can be the gospel to one another in community.

TIME

Time may be the most valuable commodity in our culture today. With the speed of information and the demands of work and home, we are running out of time. There is competition for every minute of our days. Yet, contrary to popular sentiment, we are not victims of time. The majority of time-oriented barriers to community are self-imposed. We do have a choice in how we spend our time. We are enslaved to obligations that are only enforced by our own expectations and choices.

These choices are a reflection of our priorities. If we took the average household and assessed their priorities by the use of their time, most of us would be embarrassed. Where would God rank in relationship to entertainment or recreation? Where does community rank on your list of priorities? A transformational community is one that puts a premium on people. It is a community that has been laid bare by the penetrating truths of God's Word and his lavish grace, and its members are desperate to share that grace with others.

As we think about the rhythm of time within our community groups, we need to shepherd one another to a redeemed view of time and our priorities while understanding the cultural barriers regarding time. In other words, we need to be able to find a balance between considering our demands on time and providing opportunities to align our use of time with our gospel-centered priorities.

In terms of considering the demands of time, we need to be intentional about the when, how long, and how often we gather as a community. We must understand how our choices create barriers or build bridges. Traditional small groups are one-dimensional in their use of time, often meeting once a week for two to three hours. This can be a burden for the host of the group and exhausting for its members week after week. Could we achieve the same objectives—and be more life giving—by meeting for less time more frequently? Providing multiple opportunities that are optional rather than obligatory gives each member of the community, as well as potential guests, a chance to make decisions regarding their time.

So, think about the current barriers your group faces regarding time, and don't be afraid to make changes to your group's rhythms. Take children, for example. If a community group is in a neighborhood with lots of families, then the times when it meets should reflect the natural rhythms of families. Having groups who begin at 7:00 p.m. on a weekday and get done at 9:00 or 10:00 p.m. is going to be a barrier for families. Weekends, however, may be much more attractive to families for group gatherings than they would be to single folks.

Another consideration related to time is the duration of gatherings. Again, traditional groups generally meet once a week for two to three hours. That may be a burden for some folks in your group or those who have never been part of a church small group. If you want a helpful perspective on this, ask the hosts of your group. They should have a good vantage point on the demands of long groups on themselves and guests. It may be more natural and more inviting to have more opportunities of shorter duration than one long meeting a week.

After all, if community is truly a lifestyle, then it will not be relegated to one night a week. This does not mean that every opportunity is mandatory or obligatory. Rather, you use your time intentionally to be a part of the community. For example, attending a church service together is an opportunity for a rhythm that takes no additional time but provides a chance to worship together as a community. I am always surprised at how many community groups don't take advantage of this opportunity. It costs nothing in terms of time, yet is a great way to reinforce a sense of belonging to one another. But we will talk more about this later.

As we consider the idea of new wineskins, we can begin to open our eyes to the new possibilities with regard to time. Groups do not always have to meet on Tuesday nights. They could gather in the morning, during the day, or even on weekends. You have the freedom to build your group rhythms in any way that facilitates the making of disciples and accomplishing the mission of God.

As a community group pastor, I have heard every excuse for why people just can't commit to being in community. By far the most often repeated excuse is that they just don't have the time. Every time I hear that excuse, I think of a conversation that had a profound effect on me and stirred me to a holy discontent for the church.

Last year a colleague of mine, who was overseeing the youth ministry at the time, came to me with an exciting opportunity for engaging culture near our campus. While scouting a location at a local park for a picnic event, he was approached by some young men. They were eager to find out if my friend and his companions were at the park to play Ultimate Frisbee. After discovering that they were not, they invited them to join anyway. Having an agenda for the day, my colleague gracefully declined, and the young men continued to walk the park to find more players and gather any newcomers to their game. After a few minutes of scouting, the guys returned to my friend to make sure they knew they were welcome to play. After all, just because they didn't come intending to play, they were at the park now, and the group had plenty of room for some new players. As they talked, the Frisbee players explained how their group meets at the park twice a week, every week, to play Ultimate and hang out afterwards. They had been doing this for several years and are always meeting new people to draw into their community from stragglers in the park.

I found this fascinating. I was excited that the youth leader understood the concept of participating in these types of events instead of creating our own "church version." This is precisely what it means to engage the culture and build relationships so that we can show the love of Christ in our community. This was a perfect opportunity to put these ideas into practice.

But something hung with me from the description of his encounter that I couldn't shake—it was the zeal of those Frisbee guys. They had real passion and commitment. I mean, this was just a plastic Frisbee, yet these guys were willing to proselytize complete strangers proclaiming the glory of their game and the joy of their community built around it. Are you kidding me? In his book *The Shape of Faith to Come*, Brad Waggoner asked 2,500 churchgoers if they had shared the gospel with someone in the last six months, and 1,425 had not. Only 725 had done so more than once.[2] I was floored. It brought me to tears to think that these young men had more passion and excitement for a Frisbee than we do for the Savior of the world.

Common wisdom among church leaders is that in today's world you cannot expect your people to participate more than twice a week in church activities. That is to say that if you have a Sunday service, you should only expect participation in one more event, such as mid-week programming or a small group. People won't give more time in today's busy world. Yet here was a group of people willing to come together in community around a plastic disc twice a week for years. It put me to shame. It put the church to shame.

I am often confronted with the claim that a person is not active in the church community because of a lack of time. "I just don't have time right now. . . . Maybe in the next season of life." What a crock. The issue is not, and never will be, time. The issue is our desire. When our community gives us life, we will always find time for it. We will change our schedules to accommodate it, and we will want others to experience it. We must find out what is strangling the life out of our communities and begin to live in community in such a way that it brings glory to Jesus and transforms lives. When the glory of Jesus inspires passion and zeal, we will be surprised at how much time we find.

SCENE

In terms of community rhythms, the scene is simply the location and atmosphere of where you gather as a community. Considerations of scene are very important. The aesthetics of a space can have a significant impact on the dynamics of a group. In an article in *Scientific American Mind*, Emily Anthes explored the importance of space and creativity. Below is an excerpt:

> In the 1950s prizewinning biologist and doctor Jonas Salk was working on a cure for polio in a dark basement laboratory in Pittsburgh. Progress was slow, so to clear his head, Salk traveled to Assisi, Italy, where he spent time in a 13th-century monastery, ambling amid its columns and cloistered courtyards. Suddenly, Salk found himself awash in new insights, including the one that would lead to his successful polio vaccine. Salk was convinced he had drawn his inspiration from the contemplative setting. He came to believe so strongly in architecture's ability to influence the

mind that he teamed up with renowned architect Louis Kahn to build the Salk Institute in La Jolla, Calif., as a scientific facility that would stimulate breakthroughs and encourage creativity.[3]

This should not be a surprise. As image bearers of God, we are naturally inclined to recognize beauty around us, emanating from the Creator, that inspires us to our own creativity. Thus, we should be intentional about where we meet. Not only should we consider the aesthetics of a space that make it warm and inviting, we also need to consider whether the location is a bridge builder or a barrier.

The majority of community groups that I run across meet exclusively in homes. It may come as a surprise to most churched people who are conditioned to this experience, but someone's home is a very intimate location. Going into the home of someone you don't know can be very intimidating for the average person. Add to that the fact that they are going into a group of people who know each other well, and that creates a tremendous energy barrier for someone to overcome.

Building rhythms that take us into different locations with lower energy barriers will transform a community group from a navel-gazing community to one that is engaging the neighborhood around it. When community is a people and not an event, you can gather in parks, pubs, baseball games, yards, coffee shops, apartment courtyards, and so on. You can alter the scene of your group to better encourage worship, community, and mission. Take the time to think about how you could adjust your rhythms to expand the scene where you gather as a community.

SUBSTANCE

The idea of substance is tied closely with the spaces that we talked about in the previous chapter. Substance is the content of a particular discussion or gathering. Some leaders feel as though every time a group gathers it must be a soul-exposing hunt for idols in our hearts. These leaders often have the spiritual gift of rebuke. Confession and repentance are hallmarks of a Christ-centered community, but that doesn't mean that every gathering is the appropriate time for a throw down. Groups who always swim in the deep end make it hard to integrate new people into the group, especially nonbelievers.

On the other hand, some leaders are all about hanging out and small talk. They define fellowship as having fun and ignore the need to be confronted by the gospel. Most of us have experienced this type of group. We call these "nacho groups" because they just sit around eating nachos for an hour and never open their hearts to one another. Groups who spend all their time in the shallow end never experience transformation. Many people in our churches have given up on community because our promise of transformation elevated their expectations and they were met with nachos.

As we lead our groups, we need to understand what content is appropriate for a particular time and place. Leaders should be shepherding their groups to comprehend the importance of understanding the right substance for a particular gathering. If we look at the spaces in which our groups exist, we can see how substance works.

PARTICIPATION

In the space of participation, our goal is to build relationships with our neighbors. We want to genuinely hear their stories and get to know them as individuals. This is not the right time for *The Four Spiritual Laws*.[4] Pursuing relationships will provide opportunities for sharing the gospel, but this is usually not the right time or place. Relationships are fledgling at this point. Without a real relationship, you have no voice to speak into someone's life. Keep the substance of this space light until the relationship warrants a deeper conversation.

SERVICE

This space is about serving and blessing our neighbors. Rolling out a gospel presentation in the middle will feel like a bait and switch. Allow this space to be a physical presentation of the gospel as you share the love of Christ through service. Like participation, this space allows us to build relationships and grow in our genuine love for our lost neighbors. Questions about why we are serving the neighborhood will provide ample opportunity to develop deeper conversations.

HOSPITALITY

Intimacy is increasing as we get to the hospitality space. You know that relationships are growing if someone accepts an invitation into your space that allows for deeper questions about one's story and yours. Hospitality events should be considered light affairs, but they provide more opportunities to go deeper through smaller conversations.

FELLOWSHIP

Because fellowship is our deepest and most intimate space, it opens the door for deeper substance and discussion. Our relationships allow us to be vulnerable and transparent with one another. Because we have built relationships over increasing levels and depths of intimacy, we can feel safe sharing even the dark areas of our lives. When we pay attention to the appropriate levels of intimacy, opportunities arise for nonbelievers to share their lives openly, which in turn allows you to share the hope of the gospel. This doesn't mean that every fellowship gathering requires Kleenex tissue, but it does mean that this is the space for deeper conversation. The point of each of the spaces is that there are varied degrees of depth, and a healthy group should experience a variety of depth and substance. Scripture tells us that we are to "rejoice with those who rejoice, weep with those who weep."[5] Some times of deep fellowship will be fun and occasions to party. Others will be times of trial and sorrow as we walk with one another through the consequences of sin and the fall. Healthy communities must be willing to walk through both times together.

One mistake that some groups fall into is the belief that one is better than the other. Some groups are so concerned with appearing as though they have it all together that they are unwilling to dive deeply into each other's lives for fear that they may get dirty. These groups ignore the reality of life under the curse. By doing this, they provide no opportunity for redemption in people's lives. If we cannot expose our sin to the light, then we have no way of letting brothers and sisters speak the gospel into our lives where it counts.

The other extreme is the community that never comes up for air.

We cannot assume that we have not had a spiritual experience just because no one broke down weeping. These groups ignore the reality of *Christus Victor*, that Jesus has conquered Satan, sin, and death. These groups need to celebrate the resurrection and Christ's victory.[6]

As a leader, you will need to think about the tendencies of your group to traffic in particular levels of substance and shepherd them toward different experiences that are still saturated with the gospel. This will broaden their understanding of the gospel and God's grace, and will lead to a healthier, more missional community.

HEARING THE BEAT

Now that we understand a little more about the rhythms of community and are ready to try something new, we have to ask what new rhythms we ought to try. Part of owning the mission as a community group leader is becoming a student of our neighborhood. When we do this, we start to observe the natural rhythms of the culture. We can then incorporate some of those rhythms into the rhythms of our community group in order to reduce barriers and build bridges to our neighbors.

Seattle is home to the Boeing Company. Boeing is a significant employer for several neighborhoods in the north and south ends of Seattle. One of the rhythms that a community group in those neighborhoods must contend with is the work schedule for Boeing employees. To offset their schedule with traffic patterns, the typical manufacturing shift is from 6:00 a.m. to 2:30 p.m. rather than from 9:00 a.m. to 5:00 p.m. A typical 7:00 p.m. to 9:00 p.m. group would effectively eliminate the majority of families in that neighborhood. They are on a different rhythm and need to be in bed by nine to get up the next day for work. A group that observes this rhythm, however, can adjust the times when they gather to match the rhythms of that neighborhood.

As we discussed before, the idea is to be intentional and ask why we do the things we do. What are the natural rhythms in your neighborhood, and how can you begin to harmonize with them? Can you hear the beat of your neighborhood?

Everyone has a story about why it is hard to hear the neighborhood rhythms, but the reality is that very few are actually looking and listening. We are not accustomed to paying attention. The motivation to do so must again come from our love of Jesus and recognition of his grace to us. When we are aware of this, we can get pretty excited about paying attention.

Practically, to hear the beat of your community you need be in it, walking it and talking to people. Baristas, mailmen, bartenders, and store clerks are all observers of life in your neighborhood whom you see every day and probably never ask more than an obligatory, "How are you?" If you want to get to know the vibe and the rhythms of your group, ask more questions of these folks. They have a wealth of social knowledge.

If you want to build a community group that leaves a lasting gospel effect on your neighborhood, you need to make it your goal to know as much about your neighborhood as you can. If community is happening, then you should be a part of it. Join neighborhood associations and community centers. Spend twenty minutes in front of the community bulletin board and take note of the types of activities that are happening in the community. Subscribe to community newsletters and blogs. Walk your neighborhood and pray that the Holy Spirit would help you see the rhythms of your community and the opportunities to build bridges. The best leaders become students of their mission field. As you become better at observing culture and rhythms, you will be more effective in reaching people for Jesus, and you will become better at shepherding your group to become healthier disciples of Christ.

PLAYING JAZZ

Once we have a good understanding of our community rhythms, barriers, and opportunities, we can start to put these ideas together. Spaces and rhythms work together to create a new way of experiencing community. As we move away from event-centered community, we don't want to create just a different set of rigid rhythms. Rather, we want to use these concepts to inform and teach us how to live more fluid and authentic lives together.

When we are living life together, walking in the Spirit, and dedicating our daily lives to the glory of Jesus, being a part of a community group feels like playing music. It is like playing jazz. Jazz has a good deal of structure that a musician works within, but it allows for amazing creativity and freedom. Once you understand the structure and the spaces you can play in, the music can flow naturally through the instrument.

In this metaphor, traditional event-based small groups are like a series of notes. The same note is played every week at the same time. It develops a pattern but it is by no means a song. We can hit the note every time and not make music.

To help illustrate this, let's take the diagram of spaces that we looked at in chapter 6 and stretch it into a continuum. We have the same spaces but they are on a timeline.

Spaces Continuum: Traditional Small Groups

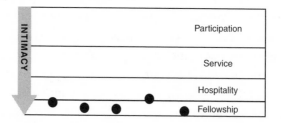

A traditional group looks like a series of separate events. Without intentionality, they exist is a small span of space and never engage the culture around them. Not only are these groups not effective in advancing the kingdom to the lost, but also they are not effective at making disciples because they are never challenged in their faith and they never participate in mission. In such a community, people live separate lives that come together only for an event once a week.

In the image below we see a picture of a group that has been intentional about providing opportunities to experience community in multiple spaces. Intentionality and a commitment to one another and the mission of God connect individual events into a rhythm of living life together. This is the goal of a gospel-saturated community group on mission.

Spaces Continuum: Community Groups

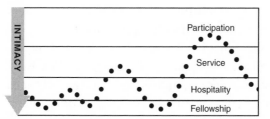

Using alternative rhythms with a gospel intentionality to reach their neighborhood, this community has begun to live life as a community rather than as individuals. Additionally, more opportunities increase the time we spend together as a group and encourage neighborhood involvement and relationships from every member.

Spaces Continuum: Harmonized Lives

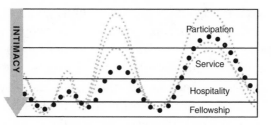

As we begin to live life intentionally around us, as Tim Chester and Steve Timmis suggest in *Total Church*, our lives begin to harmonize.[7] We begin to live in sync with our neighbors and each other.

WAFFLES FOR JESUS

Bill was convicted that although he had been a Christian for the past six years, the only way people knew that fact was by him telling them. Although his community group was dedicated to the Word and each other, it was not making an impact in their neighborhood. If they were to disappear, the only impact to the community would be the freed-up parking spaces on Tuesday nights.

Bill longed for something different, so he began to dream about how he could engage his neighbors. He thought about hosting a community barbeque, but after studying the neighborhood, that wasn't a great idea. Bill lived in a culturally diverse neighborhood where several people ran eating establishments. A barbeque would compete against their livelihoods and most would be working at that time anyway.

Few people, however, worked on Sunday, and there was not an established breakfast location nearby. Bill got an idea. He and his wife began to make waffles on Sunday mornings for their neighbors. Not your "Leggo my Eggo" waffles but gourmet waffles. Imported ingredients made these waffles a must-have. And the only place you could get them was in Bill's kitchen.

The waffles were a hit. At first a few neighbors dropped by. As the rumors about these famous waffles began to spread, Bill and his wife began to see over a hundred neighbors come through their kitchen on Sunday mornings. Bill did not require people to listen to a gospel presentation to eat a waffle; he simply loved them as Jesus loved him, with no strings attached.

As this became a rhythm of Bill's community group, they began to develop relationships that opened doors to tell people how Jesus could change their lives as he had for them. This not only changed the lives of the neighbors who ate waffles, it changed the lives of the community group itself. As they served others and became concerned about their lives and stories, they began to see the mission through the eyes of Christ. They became missionaries in their own backyards. For some it was the first time that they had participated in the Great Commission, and it was life changing.

STARTING A NEW BEAT

Introducing new rhythms into a community group that has grooved some deep ruts will take conviction and patience. The best way to start is by redeeming wasted moments that can be opportunities for community. Take the Sunday service example that I mentioned earlier. Our cultural default is to attend church as an individual or with our families. At our church, we offer multiples services, and people from a community group can choose from several times to attend services on Sunday. What a group has in common, however, is that the majority of them will attend a service on Sunday. What if we redeemed this time for community? Worship, communion, and the hearing of the Word are not experiences for individuals. These are experiences for a community of believers. This is the picture we see in Acts 2.

Additionally, as we take communion, we are called to address sin within our community before we partake. Many or most of those offenses are going to occur within our community group. How then can we address these offenses if our community is spread out through four services during the day? Making Sunday an opportunity to gather as a community for worship addresses these concerns and doubles the amount of time we spend as a community without requiring any additional time from our schedule.

Another opportunity can be found in our eating habits. Studies show that the average American goes out to eat over four times a week.[8] That's pretty amazing. How could you use that pattern to develop community? Establishing a standing reservation at a local eatery every Friday night can provide an opportunity to gather as a community at a social event that will fit into most people's natural rhythm of eating out. This not only allows us to gather as a community, but also provides a low energy barrier opportunity to invite neighbors to experience our community. It becomes a consistent hospitality event. Adding both of these opportunities can transform a community group from a collection of individuals into a community just by increasing the frequency of interaction.

If a traditional small group rhythm looks like this:

Example Week: Bible Study

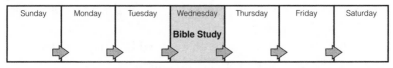

Then combining Sunday and dinner out would give us the following rhythm:

Example Week: Intentional Community

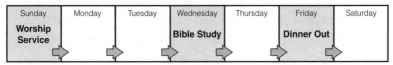

Through this rhythm we have tripled the opportunities for community and added an opportunity to invite nonbelievers into our community. This is a simple way to try out a new rhythm within your community group without demanding any more time from the people in your community.

Darrin was a community group leader who wanted to change the culture in his community group. They were used to traditional patterns of community meeting once a week and were frustrated that they were not experiencing transformation. It was life sucking and a burden, and they saw little to no growth. They were not seeing anyone meet Jesus. Embracing the ideas from this chapter, Darrin and his wife encouraged the group to start meeting before the 11:00 a.m. service to sit together, and they invited everyone in the group to come eat at a local pub on Friday night.

Some folks showed up on Sunday, but Friday night was a bomb. Not "the bomb," but a complete dud. After three weeks of little involvement, the leaders were getting discouraged. A few folks were coming, though, so they stuck with it. As that handful of people spent more time together, they began to open up and experience community with one another. Things that competed for their time seemed less important, and they began to prefer to spend Friday nights together. This feeling was contagious and began to change their community group. People opened up more during their typical community group gathering, and subsequently lives began to be transformed by the gospel.

Friday night took off and people started inviting neighbors and coworkers. Because the experience in community became life changing, they wanted others to experience it. They were no longer embarrassed to invite nonbelievers. Over the course of three months, they saw several people make commitments to Christ.

Once a group experiences this type of transformation, the work for the leader becomes fairly easy. The group begins to self-organize and the leader does not need to, nor should he, attend every group event. The group begins to develop a community orientation and opportunities multiply. It becomes life giving and life breathing as the entire community wants to replicate and share their experience.

MY COMMUNITY'S RHYTHM

At this point, you should start taking the concepts from this section to develop your own community group. As an example, let me walk you through the rhythm of my community. This is a typical week in the life of our community group. It doesn't always look like this, but this will give you a practical example of what a community group can look like.

SUNDAY

Sunday is a workday for me, but I make it a point to spend one of the four services at our campus with my family and community. We intentionally connect before the service and sit together for the worship and preaching. We generally get a chance to connect for fifteen minutes before and after the service. We usually have casual discussions, but we are ready to pray for one another if it is warranted.

TUESDAY

Tuesday is our standard gathering night. Because we have several children in our group, we have the moms come early and feed the kids at 5:00 p.m. before the dads and the rest of the group arrive at 6:00 p.m. This works well for us because it reduces the chaos of trying to feed the kids at the same time as the rest of the group. At 6:00 p.m. the kids do an activity or play while the adults eat dinner. (Having the kids play quietly near the dining room gives them a chance to hear the conversation and participate if they want.) Tonight the weather was great, so the kids played in the yard as we ate, and one of the couples in the group took a rotation of keeping an eye on them.

During dinner we try to start the discussion on the Scripture that was preached the previous week. This week the sermon was on

Luke 10:38–42, when Jesus visited Mary and Martha. The weekly curriculum had a discussion question about what typically distracts us, and Pastor Mark challenged us during the sermon to consider if we tend to be more contemplative like Mary or more active like Martha. While we started discussing the Mary/Martha question, Jen and Anne picked up on a conversation they had begun during the week. Anne had been having a hard time responding with grace to her kids and needed Jen to speak the gospel into her situation.

As we finished dinner, we moved into the living room. Jen and Anne stayed at the table to continue their conversation. The rest of us began to dig deeper into the community questions provided for Luke. As we discussed the idea of being distracted by life and neglecting our relationships with Jesus, we began to confess specific areas where this was happening in our lives. For Alison, it was the need to have the house in order and to take care of the kids. For Tim, it was the pressure of success at work. As we confessed these areas in our lives, we began to consider what it would look like to receive God's grace and spend time in his Word and prayer before letting the troubles of the day swallow our time. For some, this opened their eyes to areas of repentance they had never thought of before; for others it was a reminder of what God was already teaching them. Next week we will check in with each other to see how God met us in those moments and how it changed our hearts' inclinations throughout the day. Follow-up is important as repentance is about action, not just confession.

This is typical of our Tuesday dinners. The goal is to be flexible but gospel focused as we let conversations run their courses naturally. Each night as those conversations wind down, we spend significant time in prayer. Tonight as we moved toward this time, Jen and Anne rejoined us, and we thanked God for pursuing us in relationship and asked for his forgiveness for neglecting such a wonderful gift. Occasionally, we will use this time to sing songs together or meditate on a psalm as an act of worship. As well, we like to include the kids in this prayer time. (With young kids this may be distracting, but it is a blessing for the kids to be a part of the community.) Tonight the younger kids were a little talkative during prayer, but we saw that as an opportunity to practice our repentance of being prone to distraction. The rest of the night was casual chaos as families and individuals made their ways home.

THURSDAY

Every other Thursday we have a standing reservation at a local restaurant for happy hour. This is a completely optional time to hang out as a community. My wife and I get a babysitter for the evening and eat appetizers with the community before we head out for a date night together. This reduces the number of times we need to get a babysitter and gives us some time with friends when our attention is not divided. This provides a low energy barrier opportunity to invite friends and neighbors into our community group and get to know them personally.

SATURDAY

Inspired by the waffle idea, every other Saturday from 8:30 a.m. to 10:30 a.m. we cook breakfast for the neighborhood. We make homemade cinnamon rolls and freshly cooked crepes and have coffee donated by a local coffee shop. We put out a three-foot-tall orange fork in the yard to alert the neighbors that we will be making breakfast that Saturday and let the news spread by word of mouth. This is a way that we provide hospitality to the neighbors and serve them as well. We also look for opportunities once a month to serve the neighborhood or participate in a neighborhood event. When you put it together, our rhythm looks like this:

Example Week: Orange Fork

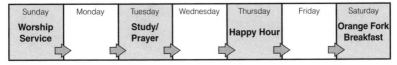

Sunday	Monday	Tuesday	Wednesday	Thursday	Friday	Saturday
Worship Service		**Study/ Prayer**		**Happy Hour**		**Orange Fork Breakfast**

Over a month, it might look like this:

Example Month

Sunday	Monday	Tuesday	Wednesday	Thursday	Friday	Saturday
Worship Service		Study/ Prayer		Happy Hour		
Worship Service		Study/ Prayer				Orange Fork Breakfast
Worship Service		Study/ Prayer		Happy Hour		Hood Event
Worship Service		Study/ Prayer				Orange Fork Breakfast

Within this rhythm are countless opportunities to be community for one another as we watch each other's kids and help with projects or spend time together outside group-organized activities. Every "event" is an optional opportunity rather than an obligation and leads us to *be* rather than to *do* community.

Other potential rhythms that you might consider could look like this:

Example Week: Midweek Dinner

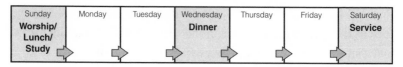

Sunday	Monday	Tuesday	Wednesday	Thursday	Friday	Saturday
Worship/ Lunch/ Study			Dinner			Service

In this rhythm, the group focuses Sunday on the Word, worship, and prayer. Most of Sunday is spent in community as the group Sabbaths together. This frees up the week for hospitality and service.

Example Week: Kids

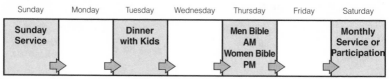

Sunday	Monday	Tuesday	Wednesday	Thursday	Friday	Saturday
Sunday Service		Dinner with Kids		Men Bible AM Women Bible PM		Monthly Service or Participation

This is a great rhythm for groups with lots of kids. The advantage is that the standard meeting is more social in nature and includes children in the community. The dinner can be scheduled for two hours rather than a four-hour marathon. The men get a morning to dig deep into Scripture and prayer. Then the dads watch the kids for the wives to gather in the evening for Bible study and prayer.

Note that all the rhythms suggested here are descriptive rather than prescriptive. As we discussed, you need to consider the natural rhythms of your life and the lives of your neighbors. Then you can develop rhythms that incorporate the elements of community in multiple spaces that are unique to your neighborhood. Reproduce these types of community groups, and you will change your city.

CATALYST

We want to be very intentional in the way that we experience community. The goal, however, is for these rhythms to be a natural and outward expression of the gospel. We want to open people's eyes to a different way of experiencing life and community because of the reconciling work of Jesus. At the beginning, making changes may start out a bit controlled, but as we experience transformational community, they will become second nature. Regimenting a new set of rhythms won't change people's hearts. Be a catalyst for change, and inspire people to a greater vision of proclaiming and advancing the kingdom. Use these ideas to equip your people with new categories of community. Point them to the glory of our amazing Savior to stir the inherent call to mission within every image bearer of God to join the fight to advance the kingdom of God.

8

STRUCTURE

ORGANIC COMMUNITY

Let's turn our attention for a moment to the structure of community groups. I have been reticent to address it up to this point because of our propensity to find a system that has success and assume it will bring success to our ministry. I remember the lesson from the movie *The Karate Kid* that knowing a few moves won't keep you from getting your rear end whooped. This structure strategy, as well as any others you read about, should come with a warning: *do not use without biblical conviction.*

The structure of community groups should be the outflow of your biblical conviction on community and the ecclesiology of the church. Considering that so few churches give significant thought to church government, it stands to reason that less thought would be given to the implications of the small group system. Unfortunately, when we neglect to build a structural foundation for our groups, they become anemic. Churches with little group structure and organization will generally have little to no growth, especially as church attendance increases. The bigger the church, the more pronounced this effect.

You may be asking, What about all this talk in recent years about organic ministry? Am I advocating cookie-cutter, regimented community? No, of course not. Actually, I am excited about the work being done to deconstruct outdated forms of community and challenge us to consider the authenticity of our lives together. Many works like *Total Church* and others are advocating for such things.[1]

They are calling us to a more natural, everyday species of community, which I applaud and with which I agree wholeheartedly.

Sometimes, however, people have a different meaning of organic. They want community that is unstructured, hands off, and free of expectation. That is not organic—that is just lazy.

The word *organic* comes from the same root as the word *organized*. The natural world is full of order. Organisms are structured at every level, from cellular makeup to social interactions. Similarly, we see the same design and attention in the structure of the church and home. It is God's grace that he has given us structures of headship and authority to organize the church. These are gifts to the church to help it be effective in transforming the lives of the saints and reaching the world for Jesus. It is impossible to read the Old and New Testaments and not see the attention to detail that God gives to the organization of the body of Christ. From the tribes of Israel to the establishment of elders and deacons in the early church, the church has operated within a structure designed to encourage the worship of God and the care of his people.

So when I advocate for natural, organic community, I am advocating for community that has enough structure to support the healthy expression of the gospel without stifling creativity and authenticity. This means that the structure should support the biblical convictions we have explored in earlier chapters while providing a platform for unique expression. Thus, as you develop your biblical conviction for your ministry and the unique mission that God has for your church, your structure may (and should) be affected. If you make a radical shift in your purpose and understanding of community but fail to change the organization of those groups to achieve that purpose, then you will probably not see the revolution you are hoping for in your groups. So let's take a look at how the structure of community should support those convictions.

THE JETHRO PRINCIPLE

Whether intentional, I see a lot of churches "fall" into community groups. By this I mean that they think groups are a good idea, and they get them rolling with little thought to a sustainable system of growth. They appoint a group coordinator who oversees all groups that naturally form. Some would consider this the budding of natural community growth and organization.

Here is the problem: if you ask a scientist what the terms "natural" and "organization" produce, they will give you the term *entropy*. Simply put: over time, systems naturally become more disorganized apart from the input of energy. In other words, the world naturally moves toward chaos unless you help it out. Think of what happens to a garden that is untended, or at recess at your local school without teachers there to maintain order. God has made us garden tenders since the beginning. Bringing order to chaos is a way in which we image the goodness of God. This is a lesson that even Moses needed to learn after God brought Israel out of Egypt.

In Exodus 18, Moses gets a visit from his father-in-law, Jethro. Moses regales him with the story of God's faithfulness when he arrives. Unfortunately, the next day, Moses is unable to hang out with him or catch a game because he is swamped at work. He has let the organization of his church develop naturally, and it's beginning to overwhelm him. He is suffering from a common ailment found among the pastoral species. Understanding his call from God to shepherd his flock, Moses assumes *he* must be the one to feed, lead, and shear every sheep. We will call this the Moses Syndrome.

Because the Moses Syndrome is a condition whereby the leader has a swollen sense of importance, you may assume that this is a condition reserved for the prideful. But remember, we are talking about Moses here. Self-proclaimed or not, it was the Holy Spirit who inspired the truth that he was "a very humble man, more humble than anyone else on the face of the earth."[2] Moses's distortion was not produced by pride, but by a calling and concern for his sheep.

His love for his sheep resulted in a structure of pastoral care that was overly dependent on him. Day after day, every argument within the church was brought to him to figure out. Every complaint, whether about the volume of the band or the level of the auditorium lighting, was brought to his desk. And this was no small-town church. Israel was estimated at five hundred thousand people at the time, and dealing with every dispute took all day and every day except the Sabbath. That's what we call a bottleneck.

Jethro points out several reasons why this type of structure is untenable. First, no man can keep up with all the problems in the church without it killing him. Second, if he is bogged down addressing every trivial issue in the congregation, then no one is leading the church forward. The captain of the ship doesn't hang out in the engine room checking the gauges. He has an engineer for that so he can drive the boat. Moses was the captain and needed to cast the vision and lead the body.

Third, when you do all the work yourself, you never develop leaders. Jethro challenges Moses to develop leaders and trust God by giving away some control. In doing so, Moses is not abdicating his responsibility. He is actually fulfilling his responsibility by multiplying his influence and leadership through godly men. When we are afraid to share ownership of our vision with others, we make a statement about the sovereignty of God. We say that although God is trustworthy and faithful, I am pretty sure that if I stop running on this hamster wheel, then it will all fall apart. An unwillingness to share leadership is as much about doubt in God and others as it is about confidence in one's own ability.

When we are unwilling to give people an opportunity to lead, we are essentially telling them that we do not trust the Holy Spirit to work through them. We rob them of opportunities to grow and become leaders. Over time, this will deplete the leadership source for our churches. Those who have been given spiritual gifts of leadership will either suppress those gifts or leave our churches for an opportunity to express them.

Observing this, Jethro gives Moses some advice. First, he tells Moses to loosen his grip on the reins a bit. Remember, Moses had just finished telling Jethro about how faithful God had been in freeing them from Egypt. God's faithfulness is marinating in Jethro's mind as he observes the leadership of Moses, and this informs his advice.

Second, Jethro tells Moses to build and equip the church to understand what it means to live for God's glory. This is why the proclamation of the Word is so essential for the health of the church. The church, as a whole, needs to be equipped with the Word to bring about transformation. Then, with proper leadership, transformation can occur through the gospel rather than being limited to the pastor's office.

This brings us to the structural advice that Jethro gives: appoint qualified men to lead and shepherd the flock. He is calling for some energy to be put into the system to keep it from becoming an overgrown garden. By organizing the church properly, all members get a chance to lead at their levels of calling, rather than being stifled. It keeps us all focused on the prize and lets us each contribute to the health and mission of the church.

As we assess the capacity of leaders in the church to lead various sizes of flocks, we can build a structure that ensures that every member is shepherded toward an identity rooted in Jesus, worship of God, community with one another, and mission toward the lost. From Jethro's picture of shared leadership, we at Mars Hill have built a community group structure that allows us to accomplish the purposes above in a scalable way. This structure is not unique in form. Like many other churches today, we employ a system of leaders, coaches, and pastors to oversee each group. Depending on the campus or church size, we have two levels of coaches, as described below. You may use different names for each role, but the principle is the same. Identify qualified leaders of various capacities to lead, and employ them to shepherd the flock God has entrusted to you.

Here are Jethro's levels of leadership as applied to community groups:

Jethro Principle Capacity Chart

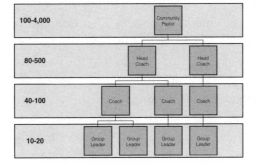

PURPOSE

As I said before, the structure that we have employed at Mars Hill Church is fairly common among small group structures. What I do believe is rather unique is the purpose of that structure. Often the driving purpose behind such a structure is management. This looks fairly similar to most corporate business structures, where management is the primary need. This is well and good in business, but it is misplaced in the church. When Jethro encouraged Moses to appoint leaders, he did so in the context of teaching them in the ways of the Lord. He wasn't advocating for managers to keep people in line. He was advocating for shepherds who knew the Word of God and could care for the sheep.

In chapter 2 we discussed the biblical purposes of community groups. We established that community is a primary vehicle for pastoral care and discipleship and an untapped vehicle for mission. If this is the case, then the structure of groups and group leadership must support these functions of community. As well, the structure will provide an administrative purpose of organization and communication.

PASTORAL CARE

Again, one of the primary functions of community groups within the church is pastoral care. Our structure has been designed to ensure that every active member of the church is shepherded by a leader, coach, or pastor. This conviction came from the observation that churches often neglect to pastor their leaders. Leaders are equipped to pour themselves out to their people but are often forgotten in the chain of care. It may be assumed that they are not in need because they have risen to leadership, but that is far from the truth. Until the return of Jesus, we all need to be shepherded regardless of our position within the church. This ensures that the pastors of the church are fulfilling their responsibilities to shepherd every member of their church and leave no leader behind.

The expectation of pastoral care also means that each level of leadership carries responsibility and delegated authority. Leaders should be equipped to shepherd and know when to escalate issues to their coach or pastor. As well, they may participate in some levels of church discipline and restoration. All in all, the structure provides a framework for shepherding the entire church rather than the few that make it into one-on-one counseling.

DISCIPLESHIP

The leadership structure provides relationships for discipleship and growth. As Pastor Bill Clem states in his book on discipleship, we want to be a church of disciples creating disciples.[3] No Christian should be a cul-de-sac. Every leader/member should be discipling someone and every leader/member should be discipled. This gives us an avenue for growth and maturation as well as leadership development within the church, allowing members to rise to the level of their calling with a variety of places to serve in the kingdom. The structure provides a network through which discipleship can naturally occur within relationships that are consistent and intentional.

MISSION

One of the purposes of the leadership structure is to implement the vision and accomplish the mission of the church. The structure is designed to promote ownership of the mission of Mars Hill Church at the group level as groups carry out the mission in their neighborhoods. We intentionally build our structure around geographic regions to emphasize the neighborhood strategy. Coaching relationships reflect context. Coaches are geographically close to their groups and the people they are trying to reach. This encourages ownership by clearly defining a missional focus for a particular leader. We talked about the accessibility of the mission in chapter 3, and it can be clearly seen in the organization of the church. Each group coach and head coach knows whom they are serving and whom they are trying to reach. When you look at this structure, you can see why having open groups with a model of replication is necessary. As groups accept the mission of God to reach their neighbors, they should be growing. This means that every group is planning for the day when they can plant a new group.

Additionally, the leadership structure provides enough over-sight to empower leaders to express community in new and unique ways. By providing a consistent structure, we have the confidence to encourage freedom in the way community is expressed in particular contexts.

ADMINISTRATION

Though less sexy than the shepherding purposes above, the structure of groups does provide some other necessary functions. A good structure facilitates communication throughout the body. It provides channels for communicating vision and values as well as needs in an efficient and effective way. It also allows leaders to be more a part of the leadership process of the church. Without such a system, leaders are made aware of issues at the same time as their group but are expected to shepherd the group through them. By keeping them in the information loop, you not only reinforce their true value to the church, but also you help them be better leaders.

Moreover, this type of organization lets issues bubble up from groups in helpful and constructive ways. Rather than issues being carried to leadership through the squeaky wheel method, they can naturally rise up through group leadership. As coaches notice patterns in the issues their groups are dealing with, they can notify the head coach or pastor to see if it may be an issue that we need to address as a corporate body. For example, if groups are consistently dealing with depression, the elders may want to do some equipping of leaders on the subject or address it in an upcoming sermon.

Lastly, even though I don't want management to be the primary motivation for a sound structure, it is important to clearly identify who is responsible for shepherding people in the church. Regardless of how you organize, whether by geography, life-stage, or relationship, you need to consider the implications of growth. How do you establish new relationships and ensure that people do not fall through the cracks? Build a system that simply defines these relationships. Relational models are notoriously bad at this and take more energy to maintain. A geographic structure makes this fairly simple while providing a clear backdrop for administering groups in an efficient and effective way.

SPAN-OF-CARE

In order for the structure we have laid out to accomplish the shepherding purposes that we just discussed, we need to understand the limitation of span-of-care. Span-of-care is the ratio of people that a leader can reasonably shepherd well. Practically, this is the number of groups that a coach can oversee. This number is extremely important to understand because as the span-of-care grows, the depth of care diminishes. It is kind of like pulling fresh taffy. It can get longer, but eventually it is going to sag and touch the floor, if it doesn't snap first. Finding the right balance is crucial to a healthy community.

When the span-of-care sags, leaders feel neglected and unappreciated. The entire structure is built on relational capital. If people feel neglected, the system goes bankrupt. Growth stalls because leaders do not feel motivated or equipped to replicate. Shepherding is reduced to management because there isn't time to develop close relationships. This leaves room for all kinds of issues to arise in marriages, finances, health, and so on. As well, it provides a poor example of the kind of shepherding you are asking of the leader. Ignore span-of-care for expediency and you will sink the ship before it sails.

In my experience, I have found that the average volunteer leader has a maximum span-of-care capacity of about six relationships. While the ideal number may vary between leaders, few are able to shepherd more than six leaders well. Larry Osborne from North Coast Church talks about this idea in his book *Sticky Church*.[4] The book offers some great wisdom on community and its ability to be an effective tool for reaching people. In it, Osborne discusses the idea that we have a finite number of relationship receptors and that we eventually tap out once those are full. While I don't agree that this is a fair argument for closing groups, I do see it as an important observation for developing deep shepherding relationships.

SCALABILITY

The last characteristic we must consider is whether the system we build is scalable. Nothing is worse than building a group's structure to reach your city and then having to reorganize it if you are actually successful. I would rather assume that we are going to be successful and build a structure that can handle significant growth. It may not be bulletproof, but the structure that we have built at Mars Hill Church has proven to be robust in the midst of uncharted growth. We had virtually the same system in place when we had forty groups as we did at four hundred.

When we had forty groups, we were organized the same way but coaches oversaw regions of the city. As we began to develop density in certain parts of the city, the coaches' scope narrowed to particular neighborhoods with oversight at the regional level by head coaches. As groups populated particular neighborhoods, we developed head coaches to lead the mission in those neighborhoods and established community pastors over each region of the city that eventually became campuses.

Let's take a moment to look at this structure's scalability. Below is a chart of the capacity of each level of leadership. In this structure we maintain the span-of-care ratios of one-to-six that we discussed earlier. On the right side of the chart is the range of the number of people you can shepherd each time you develop a leader in the role at the left. So for every group coach you develop, you can shepherd up to one hundred more people, and so forth.

Leader Capacity Chart

Role	Head Coaches		Group Coaches		Groups		People	
Community Pastor	3	6	6	36	10	216	100	3240
Head Coaches			2	6	8	36	80	540
Group Coaches					4	6	40	90
Group Leader							10	15

From this chart you can see that a head coach can oversee two to six group coaches, which equates to the oversight of eight to a maximum of thirty-six groups, or over five hundred people. That is pretty amazing considering that this is more than the average attendance at most churches in America. Furthermore, that oversight can be attained without extending the span-of-care beyond six for any leader. Now, I understand that this example is the maximum scenario and is not very likely, but having a head coach effectively overseeing upwards of two hundred people (four group coaches —> sixteen groups —> about two hundred people) is manageable and common at Mars Hill Church.

Most of us, however, do not have that large of a church. If that is the case, then the community group pastor will be functioning at the level of the head coach. For campuses and churches at that level, this chart should help you understand if you are primed for growth or preparing to stagnate. For instance, if you have twelve groups but no coaches, you are overextending the span-of-care of the overseer of your groups. Developing four coaches would give each a span-of-care of three and prime your groups for growth. Each new coach could handle three new groups for a total of twelve more, or 100 percent growth. You could grow to that size or more without coaches, but you will risk vision creep and dilution of shepherding quality. With all that said, the point is that if we believe that God uses his people to advance the kingdom, then we should have a structure for growth and shepherding that allows us to grow. Build it believing that you will succeed.

EXPECTATIONS OF A LEADER

Now that we have explored the merits of a good structure, let's turn our attention to the expectations of a leader. The expectations for a leader within this structure should reflect the convictions and purposes of the structure itself. With this in mind, there are three basic roles for which a leader at any level in the organization is responsible, which can be defined by the titles of shepherd, missiologist, and administrator. These roles reflect the purposes of the structure: pastoral care and discipleship (shepherd), mission (missiologist), and administration (administrator).

Before I describe what I mean by each of these roles, let me clarify that this does not mean that every leader must posses the ability to lead in all three areas. Rather, it is the leader's responsibility to ensure that each role is addressed within the group. In other words, a leader may possess all three or may develop a team that addresses all three. A great shepherding leader may have a member of the group own the administration role and lean on another member for understanding the neighborhood and identifying opportunities for mission. So although these roles may be shared with others, the leader is responsible to ensure that they are covered within the group. Let's take a closer look at the three roles.

SHEPHERD

Leaders are expected to care for and protect the flock in their charge by leading them toward worship of Jesus and maturity as disciples of Christ, as described in chapter 4. Leaders should have a heart to see people grow and the patience to lead them. While the other two roles may be shared, this role is difficult to delegate.

MISSIOLOGIST

Leaders are expected to lead the mission with a passion to see Jesus glorified in their cities. This means engaging the culture in your context and desiring to see people meet Jesus. But more than just a desire, being a missiologist is about getting out and interacting with neighbors and knowing your city.

ADMINISTRATOR

Leaders also need to organize and plan so that they can accomplish the mission. Poor organization can derail the most passionate zeal and the greatest intentions. Good organization, on the other hand, can help a leader be a better shepherd and more effective in advancing the kingdom. Leaders who are weak in administration can be helped immensely by finding someone with this gift to shore up their weakness.

APPRENTICESHIP

Because we place a strong emphasis on mission within our community groups, we expect to see a fair amount of growth. Growth is exciting, but with it comes the problem of developing leaders. The faster your growth, the more this becomes a problem, especially if your development process is slow.

One of the ways that we have been able to speed up the process of leadership development is to implement a culture of apprenticeship. This basically means that at every level of leadership we are committed to replacing ourselves. It would be fair to say that this is simply a discipleship model of having someone at your hip learning how to lead at that level.

We ask every group leader to formally identify an apprentice so that they can be preparing for an inevitable plant. This not only helps us develop leaders faster, it also keeps the idea of replication in the minds of the group. While not as formal, this same process happens at all other levels of leadership within the structure, from group coaches to community pastors, and creates a culture focused on developing and sending leaders.

RISK AND REWARD

One of the more common questions I get asked when it comes to leadership development is how to determine when to install a leader, a group coach, or a head coach. Mathematically, it is easy to see when it is necessary to add a leader. It is much harder to determine if someone is ready to take on the responsibility of leadership.

Making such decisions can be difficult for some and possibly too easy for others. Some pastors and leaders are too quick to give responsibility to untested individuals, while others are too reticent to share any responsibility at all. Understanding what you are looking for is key to striking a balance. When I am identifying any level of leader I look for three things: calling, competence, and character.[5]

CALLING

This is the sense that the person has a conviction from the Holy Spirit to take on a particular responsibility. Any level of leadership in the church will require some level of sacrifice and determination to persevere through messy situations. A sense of calling or conviction in the potential leader will give you confidence that you can count on them not to flake out on you when you need them.

COMPETENCE

This is simply the ability to lead at a given level. Competence is a combination of experience and success. A leader who has replicated the group multiple times has demonstrated the ability to cast vision and draw people to the gospel. This is the type of leader who may make an excellent coach and should be able to set an example that other leaders can follow.

CHARACTER

When it comes to community group leadership or coaches in the group system, the character expectations are those of deacons that are spelled out in Acts 6:1–7 and 1 Timothy 3:8–13. If you are relying on group leaders and coaches as an integral part of your pastoral care structure, then they should be considered deacons in the church.

Now in an ideal world, leaders with high marks in each would naturally knock on your door when the need arises. Unfortunately that is rarely the case. If your church is growing, then you will always find yourself in search of leaders. And you won't always have the luxury of having confidence in all three areas. You are then left with the choice to either stress the system by not installing a new leader or take a risk.

Many leaders are averse to risk, and for good reason. As a pastor, I take seriously the responsibility I have to shepherd my flock and the expectation that I will give an account for how I did. We can, however, fail to shepherd well by not taking risks, at least the right ones.

So what would be a good risk to take? When it comes to growth and risk, I like to use the example of a race car. I want to drive on the edge of control. I want to go as fast as I can without losing traction and crashing into the wall. If my tires never slip, then I am being too conservative. If I constantly fishtail, then I am being reckless, which will eventually end in a steaming pile of carnage. Knowing what risks are correctable helps us push the car to the limits and win the race.

When it comes to leadership, never take a risk on character. If you have concerns about one's character, then this person should not be considered for leadership. It will take a long time of consistency in the right direction before that person should get the green light. Leaders reproduce themselves. When you take a risk on character, you put the entire group (or groups) at risk.

So, pay attention to character. Talk to spouses, group members, and coworkers. Ask direct and pointed questions. Timidity in this area will get you in trouble, so don't be apologetic for being thorough. A good leader will understand and welcome the scrutiny. Moral failures are devastating at any level and are not worth the risk.

Competency is another story. If I am going to take a risk, it is generally in this area. Sometimes you just don't have anyone with enough experience to do the job. In that case, you may need to take a chance to see if a leader can rise to the occasion. With a good coaching structure, as I have laid out above, you can shepherd leaders and new coaches through a lack of experience. What they gain on the job will develop them faster than waiting for them to develop on their own anyway. Actually leading a group builds confidence and puts weaknesses in perspective. In such a case, you will need to be more intentional about coaching them, but the rewards outweigh the risks. The risk in a lack of competence will be mostly in the speed of development and the greater effort required.

Risk in calling is bit trickier. The biggest risk is that leaders or coaches lose interest and fail to fulfill their commitment by stepping out of the responsibility that you have given them. While not as debilitating as a moral failure, this can erode the confidence of leaders or members whom they were shepherding. It can affect the integrity of pastoral care if leaders feel their coaches let them down, and it reduces their trust in the coaching relationship. These effects can be mended over time but should be considered when taking a risk on someone who is unsure about his or her commitment to the responsibility you are giving him or her.

I purposely couch the conversation of coaching in terms of calling, rather than a job, when I am talking to a coach candidate. I want the candidate to understand the importance of being a coach within the church and feel a call to that level of leadership for a significant period of time. We ask for a two-year minimum commitment for coaches because of the relational nature of the position, but this may be a lifelong calling for some.

Let's look at an example. You have a group of twenty-five people in desperate need of an apprentice leader to replicate the group. You have three candidates that you have considered. Candidate A has expressed the desire to lead and is very eager. Candidate B doesn't feel ready, and C is not sure about taking on the responsibility. Below is how you have assessed each candidate:

Leader Candidate Risk Assessment

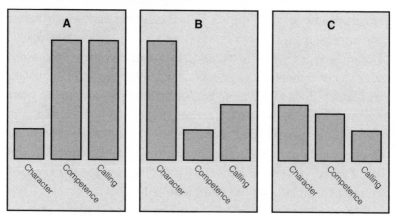

What are the risks involved with each candidate? What would you do to shepherd the group toward replication?

It may be obvious in this controlled environment, but in real world situations it is often hard to avoid choosing candidate A. The candidate has shown competence and a desire to lead and most likely has been convincing in explaining away the character concerns. But make no mistake; this person can sink the ship.

Candidate B, on the other hand, is probably the best risk to take. What the candidate lacks in experience can be addressed with coaching and on-the-job experience. As confidence is gained, the calling will become clearer. If the candidate doesn't develop, then you can put together a plan to transition him or her back out without significant damage.

In the case of C, I would encourage the candidate to consider the possibility of stepping up to leadership and give more time to develop some conviction. In a pinch, you might be able to get this candidate to help out for a short time, but you need to be ready for him or her to step out. Whether this is worth the risk is dependent on the immediate need, because you will have to do as much work later if he or she flakes. Candidate C may turn out to be a great leader with the right coaching, but it will be a bigger risk.

TRAINING

Part of building a robust structure for community includes building and equipping leaders. Think of it as a maintenance plan. When you buy a car, you expect to invest in keeping it running. If you don't, it is only a matter of time before it starts to wear down and cost you more in repairs. Don't let this part get lost as you think of building community groups within your church. A good training and equipping program will keep the system running smoothly and prevent major failures.

So what should this training look like? It can vary significantly by your context and the learning styles of your people. The number of leaders will make a difference as well. If you have ten groups, then your training program will look significantly different from that of a church with four hundred groups, which also means your training methods should adapt with growth as well.

Regardless of your context, I would encourage you to avoid a one-dimensional approach to teaching and equipping. Learning styles can vary widely. Some people learn well in lectures or classes, while others need one-on-one attention. Think through multiple ways to communicate the same message. At Mars Hill Church, our training has three major components: basic training, syncs, and coaching.

BASIC TRAINING

This is the basic DNA that we want leaders to have when they begin to lead community groups. The purpose of basic training is to establish a baseline for leaders and to ensure that every leader to whom you delegate authority to shepherd your people owns the ethos of your church. How you deliver this training can vary. In smaller campuses or churches, this may be a class or even a short-term community group of its own. Recently, due to the volume of leaders and time constraints, we have moved to self-study of material through videos and reading that apprentice leaders review with their sponsoring leader or coach. This has reduced the time demand on leaders while reinforcing their coaching relationship. The big idea of basic training is to establish the vision and expectations for leaders and ensure consistency across the board.

SYNCS

Syncs are monthly gatherings of all leaders for continuous and timely training and equipping. Bill Hybels, when talking on leaders and leadership development, often points out that vision leaks. Basically, the idea is that vision has a shelf life of about thirty days.[6] If you don't remind people of what we are doing and why we are doing it every thirty days, then they are apt to forget both. The sync gives us an opportunity each month to reinforce the vision.

As well, I have found that one of the hindrances to good coaching is the inability to schedule time together as a cohort of leaders or one-on-one time with the coaches. By providing a monthly obligation, we have reinforced those relationships and have given them space to grow. Having a time of food and fellowship as well as providing time and space for groups to gather to work out the training or discuss neighborhood strategies is very effective.

When it comes to the actual training, make it count. If you make the time worth it to your leaders, you will have consistent attendance. Each sync is an opportunity to accomplish one of three things: information, inspiration, or application.

Information is about bringing leaders into the conversation that the elders of the church are having. Community group leaders are the front-line implementers of each and every initiative we do as a church. The sync is a great way to inform them of what the leaders are working on and to elicit feedback. Inviting leaders into the conversation reinforces their value to the church and encourages them to lead out the vision.

Inspirational messages are about recasting the vision. The work of the gospel in the lives of our members, as well as reaching the lost, is hard and demanding work. Leaders need to be encouraged, inspired, and reminded of the reason we do this work: the glory of Jesus. Don't assume that because you fired up the troops with a great message last year, they are still fired up. As I said before, those embers are smoldering after about thirty days. The sync is a great place to encourage, thank, and inspire leaders consistently.

Lastly, be sure to include practical *application* during sync training. If leaders never get anything they can take home and apply, then the value of coming to a monthly gathering will diminish. Having one of the counseling pastors teach on the warning signs of depression and the steps to take as a leader is always worth the price of admission. Consider the practical situations that your leaders are facing, and use the sync to equip them to be better shepherds and missiologists.

Typical Sync Schedule
    6:00 p.m. Dinner
    7:00 p.m. Training
    8:00 p.m. Coach huddles
    9:00 p.m. Head coach huddle

COACHING

The last training vehicle to consider is the coaching relationship itself. This is probably the most valuable training vehicle at your disposal. This relationship galvanizes the other training methods when coupled with follow-up and discussion. Effective coaches will magnify any training you can provide.

To this end, invest as much time as you can in your coaches. Model the mentoring relationship and give them ownership over their leaders. Include them in counseling sessions that arise from their groups. Equip them to follow up on the basic training and to follow through on the sync training. If your coaches are equipped and empowered, then they will provide continuous and personal training for each of their leaders.

BUILDING YOUR STRUCTURE

The goal of this chapter has been to open your eyes to the importance and potential of a well-thought-out structure for community groups. A good structure not only allows you to accomplish the goal of making disciples, it can actually be a tool that helps you. A poor structure, on the other hand, can be an annoyance that you constantly trip over and that hinders growth. As you consider the structure of your groups, ask the following questions:

1. Does the structure of our groups flow out of biblical convictions?
2. Does the structure reinforce those convictions?
3. Will the structure survive success?
4. Are we primed for growth or limited by our structure?
5. Are the expectations for our leaders aligned with our purpose?

These questions should help get you started building a structure for community that facilitates accomplishing the goals you have set. By aligning the structure with the purposes of community groups, we can remove unwanted roadblocks to a community that loves Jesus, cares for one another, and effectively carries out the mission of God.

TREATMENT: EFFECTING CHANGE IN YOUR GROUPS

The purpose of this section is to equip you to effect change in your ministry in order to align with the convictions and vision that God has formed for you throughout this book. The first two sections were intended to stir up within you a holy dissatisfaction with the state of community. This section aims at helping you advance toward life-giving community.

Comedian George Carlin once said, "I put a dollar in one of those change machines. Nothing changed."[1] Reading a book can feel much like putting a dollar in a change machine. While it arouses our affections for change, it does not effect change without action.

As we begin to form a plan for rebuilding the community of the church, it is important that we start at the right spot. Some teachers have suggested that thriving community is a few simple steps away, intentionally or unintentionally implying that what we need to develop healthy community lies within a catchy new system or program.

Let me be up front with you and tell you that if it is worth achieving, it is not going to be easy. Transformational, life-filled community in a culture of quick fixes is hard to come by. Effecting change will take commitment, hard work, and patience. Changing the culture of community in your church will require a consistent plan that starts with repentance on the part of the church and dependence on the Holy Spirit to impart change in our hearts.

If you want to change the culture of community within your church, you are going to have to count the cost. But the result—a Jesus-glorifying, transformational community that is a source of life—is well worth the price. As Saint Augustine said, "If you would attain to what you are not yet, you must always be displeased by what you are. For where you are pleased with yourself there you have remained. Keep adding, keep walking, keep advancing."

9

REPENTANCE

GRACE IN VAIN

One evening as I was preparing a message for our community group leaders and thinking about the thousands of members that were participating in our groups, I kept thinking about these words from 2 Corinthians, "*We appeal to you not to receive the grace of God in vain. For he says, 'In a favorable time I listened to you, and in a day of salvation I have helped you.' Behold, now is the favorable time; behold, now is the day of salvation.*"[1]

Do not "receive the grace of God in vain." These words have a way of haunting me. What does it mean for the church to receive the grace of God in vain? Paul makes this appeal after laying out the ministry that God has for his church:

> Therefore, if anyone is in Christ, he is a new creation. The old has passed away; behold, the new has come. All this is from God, who through Christ reconciled us to himself and gave us the ministry of reconciliation; that is, in Christ God was reconciling the world to himself, not counting their trespasses against them, and entrusting to us the message of reconciliation. Therefore we are ambassadors for Christ, *God making his appeal through us*. We implore you on behalf of Christ, be reconciled to God. For our sake he made him to be sin who knew no sin, so that in him we might become the righteousness of God. Working together with him, then, we appeal to you not to receive the grace of God in vain. For he says, "In a favorable time I listened to you, and in a day of salvation I have

helped you." Behold, now is the favorable time; behold, now is the day of salvation.[2]

Not only are we reminded of what Jesus has done for us, we are also called to be his ambassadors to the world. Does it ever take your breath away that God declares that he is making his appeal through us? The Creator of the universe who can call on the trees and rocks to cry out in praise of his glory has chosen to reconcile the world through the lives and appeals of his people. Paul says that we have been entrusted with the message, the good news, the gospel, to participate in the reconciliation of our neighbors, our coworkers, our friends, our family, and even our enemies. Let the weight of Paul's statement linger with you.

For me, these words are exciting and concerning. They excite me because I can see what the community of God, empowered by the Holy Spirit, can accomplish for the kingdom. They concern me because I do not see the urgency in the church that such a lofty expectation should arouse. We cannot be satisfied with community that is unaffected by the grace of God.

Paul says that he endures "everything for the sake of the elect, that they also may obtain the salvation that is in Christ Jesus with eternal glory."[3] In 1 Corinthians he states that he has become "all things to all people, that by all means I might save some."[4] He is willing to do anything for the hope that one more person would give their life to Jesus.

Where is that passion among the church? Most Christians aren't willing to endure an awkward moment for the sake of the elect. Yet God has willed that his church, the body of Christ, should be the expression of his glory that transforms the nations. If that is the case, then something must change. We must rethink what it means for us to be the church in light of the grace we have received.

REBUILDING THROUGH REPENTANCE

George Whitefield said, "True repentance will entirely change you; the bias of your souls will be changed, then you will delight in God, in Christ, in His Law, and in His people."[5] The change that we long for will not come about with the implementation of a new system or vision for groups. We need the bias of our souls to change. We long to see our hearts realigned to delight in God, in Christ, in his law, and in his people. This kind of change starts with repentance. As we repent of the sin and disbelief that have corrupted our communities and sidelined us from the mission of God, our hearts will be prepared for a new vision. This repentance looks like a people receiving the gospel and living out of their identity as a holy nation. Change will begin with repentance.

Scripture gives us many examples of how change is effected through repentance. As the people of God turn to him and repent, he is quick to forgive and to bless. This gives a great blueprint for our own journey toward life-giving community.

Exodus 34:6–7 is the first time that God self-discloses truth about his nature to us. In this disclosure, God begins with mercy and grace. The contrast between the consequences of sin for four generations and his steadfast love for thousands of generations is telling. It shows us that God is rooting for us. He is on our side. He is predisposed to grace, mercy, and forgiveness when we are humble and repentant.

Below are a few examples of missional repentance found in the Bible. By *missional* repentance, I mean that they are examples of where the repentance of God's people led to the advancement of God's kingdom and the proclamation of his glory (in other words, our mission).

Examples of Missional Repentance in the Old Testament

1. Jacob (Genesis 35)
2. Moses (Exodus 32)
3. Samuel (1 Samuel 7)
4. Elijah (1 Kings 18)
5. Jehoshaphat (2 Chronicles 20)
6. Hezekiah (2 Chronicles 30)
7. Josiah (2 Chronicles 34)
8. Isaiah (Isaiah 6)
9. Jeremiah (Jeremiah 1)
10. Zerubbabel (Haggai 1; Zechariah 1)
11. Ezra and Nehemiah (Nehemiah 8)

Examples of Missional Repentance in the New Testament

1. Peter's sermon at Pentecost (Acts 2)
2. Paul's message in Athens (Acts 17:16–34, especially v. 30)

3. John's revelation of Jesus's words to his churches (Revelation 2–3)

In the examples above we see the importance of repentance as a first step to change. Leaders whose eyes were opened by the Word of God through the Bible or the warnings of prophets began reform with repentance. That repentance was often personal as well as corporate.

Josiah, for example, was a young king of Judah who set out to refurbish the house of the Lord. During the remodel, they came across the Book of the Law that had been all but lost to the nation of Judah. When Josiah heard the Word of God, he was mortified. Broken by his sin and the sins of his people, he sought out the Lord. God responded, saying, "Because your heart was tender and you humbled yourself before God when you heard his words against this place and its inhabitants, and you have humbled yourself before me and have torn your clothes and wept before me, I also have heard you."[6] Repentance started in Josiah's heart as he realized that they had been living in unbelief of who God is and who they were as his people.

As we prepare to change the direction of community groups in our churches, we must take time to look at what God has called the church to be. Where we have missed the mark, we should follow the example of Josiah and lead our people in repentance. This repentance begins with receiving the grace of God and believing the truth of who we are and what Christ has done. When we are humbled by his kindness, it prepares our hearts for renewal. We begin to walk in the Spirit rather than our own strength.[7] In other words, we cannot just simply try harder. You won't get there through a new initiative. God wants our hearts. He wants us to trust in him alone. We can call out to him as our Father and ask for help. As Exodus 34 points out, he is ready to respond in love.

TRAJECTORY OF CHANGE

Therefore, the path to transformative community does not begin with a new system or structure, but through repentance. What ails the church is a heart condition. If we are going to effect change, we must understand the nature of our sickness. Richard Baxter, the old

Reformed pastor, gives us sage advice for shepherding our people well. He wrote,

> We must labour to be acquainted, not only with the persons, but with the state of all our people, . . . what are the sins of which they are most in danger, and what duties they are most apt to neglect, and what temptations they are most liable to; for if we know not their temperament or disease, we are not likely to prove successful physicians.[8]

We have built systems and programs to address the need for better administration and to help people lead better Bible studies. We have also built tools to help them engage with their neighbors, hoping for a change of heart. Granted, all of these are useful in building a transformational community, but if we fail to diagnose and treat the underlying heart condition first, then these tools are little more than an iron lung keeping our groups alive.

These systems and programs effectively mask the real condition and give us a false sense of accomplishment. We can be content that our ministry is growing without taking the time to see if that growth is real or artificial. Baxter calls us to know our bodies better. By knowing our bodies we can address the heart condition and breathe life back into our churches. Then the tools and systems become weapons in the fight for God's glory rather than smoke and mirrors used to project our own.

Consider the message to the church at Ephesus recorded in Revelation:

> I know your works, your toil and your patient endurance, and how you cannot bear with those who are evil, but have tested those who call themselves apostles and are not, and found them to be false. I know you are enduring patiently and bearing up for my name's sake, and you have not grown weary. *But I have this against you, that you have abandoned the love you had at first.* Remember therefore from where you have fallen; repent, and do the works you did at first. If not, I will come to you and remove your lampstand from its place, unless you repent.[9]

What is unnerving about this rebuke is how many things the Ephesians were getting *right*. They were patient and enduring. Their doctrine was sound, and they were championing the name of Jesus. Yet they were rebuked with the threat of losing their access to the grace of God.

Why? The answer lies in their hearts. If we look at Paul's letter to the Ephesians, we see it is laced with love: love for Jesus, love for one another, and love for the world to whom Jesus is being made known through his church. Somewhere along the way the Ephesians forgot the point of their endurance and patience.

Were they no longer left breathless by the breadth and length and height and depth of Christ's love? Did they become more concerned with doctrine than unity? Were they more interested in staking their claim to salvation than making the manifold wisdom of God known to the lost?

Maybe it was one of these reasons; maybe it was all of them. What we do know is that the cure for their ailment is repentance. God is not condemning them in Revelation 5. He is giving them another opportunity to change before it is too late. God is extending grace and mercy. He is calling them to repentance.

Like the Ephesians, the beginning of our journey together toward life-giving, transformational community within the church must start with repentance. Our Father in heaven is patiently suffering our neglect. He is extending grace and giving us another chance. If, however, we do not respond, we should not expect to escape the fate of the Ephesian church.

We need to restore our first love. Because Jesus first loved us, this is simply a response to his grace. We receive his love, embracing our identity as his people, and reject all challengers for his worship. Then, as we trust in him, we let the Holy Spirit restore our hearts that have become barriers to our participation in the mission of God.

SEEING IS BELIEVING

Repentance began for me when I opened my eyes. Though dated, the movie *The Matrix* still provides a great image of the church today.

While Neo is sleeping soundly and imagining an average but peaceful existence, a war is waging all around him. However, he is oblivious to this fact because, unknown to him, he is asleep. By an external provocation he is offered a chance to wake up, but he must choose to leave the only reality he knows. If he takes the blue pill, he continues to sleep and experience life in the dream. If he takes the red pill, his eyes will be open to the dirty and dangerous, but very real world. It won't be pretty or easy, but it will be true.

I was preparing for our monthly training when I was overcome by a wave of discontentment. That night I would lay out another great tool for making the lives of my leaders easier. It would reduce the administration time for them as they led their groups. As I sat there, I started to think about the thousands of people we had in community groups around the Seattle area. I thought about the millions of unsaved and dying people in our city.

I was broken that I had been settling for building a ministry rather than being moved by the work of Jesus. I was lulled into believing that the number of groups I had developed at Mars Hill was my measure of success. I had equated being in a community with being discipled. Yet, very few of those in community groups were participating in the mission of God, few were even fighting against sin in their own lives, and few lived as a community of believers. They had the appearance of life, and I had enabled them to be content with appearances. Something needed to change. My eyes had been opened, and I wanted more for our community groups.

If we want to build community within the church through groups who are passionate about Jesus and produce transformation in the saints and the lost, then we must open our eyes to the reality of the battle. Many people in the church today have been given a glimpse of the real battle through the faithful preaching of the Word and the work of their pastors and leaders. Unfortunately, despite the pleas to enter into the fray and join our King in battle, many have chosen to take the blue pill.

Jesus said that he did not come to bring peace but a sword.[10] That may come as a surprise to some. We have built a Christianity that doesn't require us to take up arms. Yet, like Timothy, we have been entrusted with the message of reconciliation so that we would "wage the good warfare."[11] Our fight is against sin that wages war against our flesh, and we fight for the lives of the lost who are being devoured in the world. We have been given the weapons of righteousness that we would join in the battle for the glory of God.[12] Yet so few of us are fighting.

I want to call you and your community groups to take up arms. It is time that we opened our eyes. We cannot be content with a church full of sleeping soldiers. If we fail to rise up and declare the love of Christ, who will? Make no mistake, God is jealous for his glory. When the people of God refused to take the Promised Land, he sent them to die in the desert and raised up another generation to fulfill his purpose.[13] The Ephesians endangered their lampstand by abandoning their love and passion for the glory of God. His purposes will be fulfilled with us or despite us. I would prefer the former.

I want to be in the generation that receives the Promised Land. I want to be the faithful generation that takes up the weapons of righteousness and is willing to endure all things for the sake of the elect. I pray that the church will choose to open their eyes, acknowledge the battle, and join the fray.

Seeing the battle is essential to repentance. Once we see it, responding comes as a natural outworking of what Christ has done in us. When we called the community groups at Mars Hill to open their eyes, we saw a dramatic effect. Groups began to live their lives together with transparency and grace, leading to a reclamation of freedom and joy. As they embraced who they were in Christ, they began to see their world with the eyes of God. With eyes open to the battle around them, they began to engage with their neighbors. Groups started talking to their neighbors and listening to their stories. Some reached out to street kids and prostitutes to offer hope to a broken world through Christ. In other words, they joined the fray.

But it was not simply our blindness that kept us from the fight. There were some big hurdles that we had to get over before these stories became reality. As Baxter points out, there are some common sins that keep us from living missional lives. As a pastor over community groups, the three I see that cripple the mission the most are *apathy*, *indifference*, and *fear of man*.

APATHY

One of the most insidious sins of the church today is apathy. It is a passive sin of omission and therefore it doesn't get much press. But it is a silent killer of passion and is the antithesis to the gospel. Apathy is indifference to sin and its destruction in our lives and in the lives of others. It is an unholy contentment with the status quo. You might say apathy is the intentional closing of our eyes to the carnage on the battlefield.

John Owen said, "Be killing sin, or it will be killing you."[14] Apathy toward sin is suicide. Peter tells us that sin is waging war against our souls. As a pastor, I have personally seen the devastation caused by porn, infidelity, divorce, greed, and other forms of idolatry. Are you seeing the destruction of sin in your community? If you don't see it, open your eyes.

Scripture says that Satan prowls around like a lion waiting to devour believers.[15] Jesus teaches us that Satan is active and fighting against the expansion of the gospel.[16] Paul describes Satan as scheming, setting traps, and looking for footholds to thwart gospel transformation in our lives.[17] I guarantee that our enemy is not apathetic to the battle. People are getting slaughtered all around us, inside and outside the church. Pastors are disqualifying themselves, wives are leaving their husbands, and husbands are coveting two-dimensional women. We medicate with drugs, entertainment, and sex—and so it goes, on and on down a path of destruction.

Instead of killing sin, we often try to manage it. We manage things that we don't believe are dangerous. A new puppy is cute but mildly destructive. In order to protect our home, we relegate the young rogue to the washroom and garage where we can manage the amount of damage he can do. We are resigned to the fact that we may lose a sneaker or two, but we have it under control and can make adjustments as the puppy grows.

This is how many of us see sin, as a mischievous puppy to be managed, as if we can control it with a firm tone. The problem is that sin is not a puppy but a small fire. Spurgeon posits that managing sin is like setting a small fire and attempting to control it with the sound of your voice.[18] Sin that is not destroyed will set the whole house on fire. Apathy diminishes our view of sin and sets us up for an inferno. And if we are engulfed by sin, we will spend the war in the M*A*S*H tent rather than on the battlefield.

Such apathy debilitates community. But we don't have to live this way. The old has passed away. We are new creations in Christ, set free from sin and free to worship Jesus in spirit and in truth. We can walk in transparency with one another because our identity is secure in Christ and our sin has been crushed on the cross.

INDIFFERENCE

Finding our identity in Christ is essential because when we become apathetic to sin in our lives, it not only destroys us individually, but it also destroys our witness to the world. When the church fails to address sin, it is hard to argue for the transforming power of the gospel. But here is the cunning of apathy: we may not even care.

How is it that we drive by our neighbors to and from work every day and never consider how we might make the appeal for them to be reconciled to God? Surely we believe that Jesus is "the way, and the truth, and the life," and that through him and him alone can we be reconciled to the Father.[19] If we possess the good news and we acknowledge that the only alternative is eternal destruction,[20] then how is it that we have little passion for sharing the gospel?

How many people have given their lives to Christ within your community group this year? How many nonbelievers have participated in community with your group? If the answer is none (as it usually is when I ask these questions), then doesn't the evidence indict us of being indifferent toward the mission of God? We need an urgency for the gospel.

Indifference is often a symptom of the love of life. As John writes, "Whoever loves his life loses it, and whoever hates his life in this world will keep it for eternal life."[21] When we are more consumed with our stuff and our comfort than the advancement of the kingdom, we have chosen to keep our eyes closed. Scripture uses the images of war and harvest for participation in Jesus's mission.[22] War requires us to put our lives on the line. Harvest requires us to get dirty and work. Neither is comfortable. Neither is easy.

We cannot hang on to temporal things and make a kingdom impact. We cannot serve two masters. We must hold our lives and their comforts in an open hand for the service of our king.

God has chosen you and your community to be the message bearers, and the consequences are eternal. This may seem daunting because we have become accustomed to letting the leaders of the church do all the heavy lifting. Imagine your pastor harvesting a field. Picture him swinging a sickle as sweat beads up on his brow. He loves Jesus and is determined to harvest the crops of his Father. As you look closer, you notice that he is straining harder than he ought because he is dragging a wagon behind him. In the wagon is the rest of the church. Instead of helping, they are watching from the wagon. This is the picture I often see in the church. Pastors are breaking their backs for the mission of God while we sit back and watch.

But imagine for a moment if we all got out of the wagon and grabbed a sickle. Imagine what we could accomplish for the kingdom if we joined in the work together. Could you transform your town or city? Could you impact a generation?

The good news is that the crops are ready to be harvested. If we can lead our community groups to turn from indifference, then we will find that the fields are ripe for the harvest.[23] Jesus encourages us that he has already prepared them. He is just looking for workers who are willing to get dirty. Jesus came to save sinners,[24] and he has chosen us to make the appeal to the world. If we repent of our indifference, we can experience the joy of being a part of accomplishing his plan of reconciliation.

Repentance here starts with rejoicing in our salvation. It is gratitude and thankfulness for God's holiness and mercy. It looks like compassion for our dying neighbors. Repentance is living with a passion for Jesus and a desire to see people worship him. If we can kill indifference, we will remove another barrier to transformational community.

FEAR OF MAN

Although apathy and indifference are strangling the church, these are not our only enemies. Another barrier that is crushing the church and crippling the mission is fear of man. We fear rejection, mockery, and the loss of status among our neighbors and coworkers.

While I struggle with this sin more than apathy in my own life, I find it borders on the edge of ridiculous. The vast majority of the church in twenty-first-century America has little to fear for their faith. Mockery and rejection are of little consequence to our lives, yet this fear chokes out our faith in the resurrection and the power of the Holy Spirit. There are some Christians today who still face death for their faith, but chances are, you are not one of them. So what is it that we fear?

Jesus tells us not to "fear those who kill the body but cannot kill the soul. Rather fear him who can destroy both soul and body in hell."[25] Jesus is essentially telling us that it is ridiculous to fear anyone other than God—even if they can kill you. When we fear men or their opinions, we elevate their importance above our King's. When we are unwilling to share the truth of our Savior for fear of rejection, we do the same thing.

Do you fear God? Every instance of fear of man in the Bible leads to sin. Conversely, Psalms tells us that "the fear of the LORD is the beginning of wisdom."[26] Repentance is humbly submitting our lives to Christ and his service. It means boldly sharing our lives and faith with our neighbors.

As Paul exhorts Timothy, I want to exhort you, "For this reason I remind you to fan into flame the gift of God, which is in you through the laying on of my hands, for God gave us a spirit not of fear but of power and love and self-control."[27] We have not been given a spirit of fear but a spirit of confidence in our heavenly Father. Notice it is a spirit that he gives us. We don't need to muster confidence from within; we only need to accept the gift.

If there is something to fear, it should be the wrath of God for those who are not justified through the cross. We should be compelled by fear for our unbelieving neighbors to appeal to them to be reconciled to God. The blood of Jesus is thicker than rejection, mockery, or even death. When we see God clearly, there is nothing to fear from men. As I said at the beginning this chapter, I fear receiving the grace of God in vain. If we lived with that fear, we would never be afraid to join the battle for God's glory.

A BRIGHTER FUTURE

Just writing about apathy, indifference, and the fear of man is breaking me again as I see my shortcomings in every sentence. How about you? Are you feeling broken yet? There isn't a time when any of us are doing all the right things, myself included. But if we're honest about our failings and turn to Christ, he liberally accepts us and will empower us for ministry again. The good news is that we have died to sin.[28] Our sin has been hung on the cross. We are free to live as the chosen people of God. He restored us to himself while we were still rebelling against him,[29] and he is faithful to restore his church once again. I am not asking you to become something new. I am calling you to recognize and believe in who you already are. Christ has already done the work, and we get to joyfully receive it and reflect it to our neighbors.

Ultimately, the point is that the best strategy and a perfect structure will not produce transformational community. Authentic change is a reorientation of our hearts toward God. Everything else in this book hinges on this heart change. Life comes from God. Life in our community groups cannot be manufactured. It is received through the Holy Spirit as we abide in our Savior.

The truth is that shepherding people to authentic community is in and of itself a battle. We will need to fight against apathy, indifference, and fear of man continuously as we shepherd one another toward a bigger vision of community. But we fight by believing the truth and promises of the gospel. This is a battle that can not only be won, but also one that has already been won on the cross. We possess everything we need to live lives of holiness.[30] We have access to the great Counselor, the Holy Spirit.[31] We have the example of Jesus; we are new creations in Christ who are no longer bound to sin but are slaves of righteousness.[32] We don't have to see our lampstand removed.

We began this chapter looking at Paul's letter to the Corinthians and focused on his warning of receiving grace in vain. When we heed that warning, we run smack into the promise that "now is the favorable time; behold, now is the day of salvation."[33] What a word of hope! On the day of Pentecost, the Holy Spirit parlayed one faithful community group into a megachurch. What could he do with us if we lived with what John Piper calls "a wartime lifestyle and a hazardous liberality"?[34] Today is a favorable time as we await the return of our Savior. There really is no time like the present.

So if we want to see change in our community groups, we must start with repentance as God initiates with grace and we respond. Repentance is a restoration of who we already are in Christ, a holy people loved by our heavenly Father. It is the beginning of new life. Repentance makes way for a new vision and prepares our community groups to be used by God.

10

BOOT CAMP

BOOT CAMP

For most of you, what I have laid out in the previous chapters is probably a significant departure from how you have led community groups in the past. Implementing such changes will not happen overnight and will require good shepherding of your people. If you are leading more than a handful of groups, you will need to put together a strategy and a plan for leading people to see a new vision for community groups.

This chapter will walk you through the process we used when we implemented this vision. As you prepare your training, make it your own. Use this as a framework, and let God direct you to build groups that are transformational and life giving. In order to make such a dramatic shift in community thinking, you are going to need a good delivery system. This content is a real paradigm shift for most leaders. It isn't a bomb you can drop and watch everyone snap to it. You will need to shepherd them to understand the theology, philosophy, and practice of it.

Such shepherding will require time and consistency. You will need time to walk your leaders through the process of change, and consistent time over several weeks to galvanize these thoughts and ideas before they will own them. One way to accomplish this is to develop a boot camp for leaders.

At Mars Hill, our community group boot camp focused on mission in particular, as this was the most glaring problem within our groups. We had become complacent with insular groups who did not engage the culture. Because this is a consistent issue within community groups across the country, I thought it would be helpful to walk you through our boot camp to give you an idea of how to lead your groups to a bigger vision of community.

The boot camp consisted of seven consecutive weeks of two-hour meetings between services on Sunday. This gave us fourteen hours with our leaders in two months to walk through changes and solidify the vision. The concentration of time was very important. The longer you spread out such change, the more the vision leak that can occur.

You may want to do a retreat off site to institute such changes. This may be a good strategy, as it will give you more time and a controlled experience. However, the week in between each session was valuable time to get leaders out into their actual neighborhoods. If you are going to try a retreat, you will have to contend with the loss of this opportunity. In the end, do what works best for your leaders and your context. Here are some things we learned that we feel are keys to a successful boot camp:

MAKE IT COMPELLING

Don't waste people's time. If you are going to ask them to sacrifice a weekend, or fourteen hours over two months, make sure you have a clear plan and well-thought-out use of that time. Clearly define your vision and trajectory for the boot camp. If people know what to expect and can see the path to get there, they will be excited to give up time to be a part of it. The key to making the content compelling is prayer and dependence on the Holy Spirit. I will be sharing with you the plan we used for our boot camp, but you must own your own vision. Pray and seek wisdom for your congregation and what God wants to do in and through them. That is what will be compelling.

MAKE IT NECESSARY

Raise the bar of expectation. Give adequate time for leaders to adjust plans, but this needs to be a priority for leaders. As we discussed in chapter 9 on repentance, you have to be willing to let some leaders opt out. Not every leader will turn the corner with you, and you need to see that as God's grace. If they are not willing to embrace the vision God has for your church, then why would you want them leading some of his sheep? You will generally move as fast as your slowest leader. You can slow the entire team, or you can cut loose those who are not on board. I pastorally suggest the latter for your sanity and the good of the gospel.

REINFORCE THE VISION

Organize the boot camp in such a way as to reinforce the vision. We organized groups of leaders by neighborhood so that leaders and coaches were working together within their coaching relationships. This also forces your groups to be organized with the right span-of-care. If you need to add coaches or rearrange coaches to fit the neighborhood strategy, this is a great time to implement those changes. The boot camp provides several consistent weeks for new relationships to develop and gain momentum.

MAKE IT INTERACTIVE

Don't just preach at your leaders. Good content is important, but your people must interact with it and be able to articulate it for themselves. In most cases, you will be counting on these leaders to recast the vision to their groups. This builds ownership in the vision and requires them to understand it clearly. By making the boot camp interactive, you will give them time to process and internalize the vision. So don't set up the room as though the boot camp is a lecture. Allow leaders to sit around tables for times of discussion and building plans. Have plenty of time for questions and group discussion. Create space for leaders to rearticulate what they have heard, and provide a place for them to practice.

Additionally, a good teaching trajectory for a boot camp begins with a strong articulation of vision. Then, as you advance toward launching leaders on mission, you will need to reduce the presentation of philosophical ideas and increase the opportunities to put those ideas into practice.

Boot Camp Content Trajectory

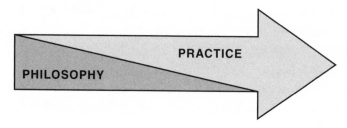

MAKE IT PRACTICAL

You will need to get from theology and philosophy to application. The purpose of the boot camp is to get leaders to own the mission of God. Talking about it is not ownership. You want to get leaders on the ground in their neighborhoods. You want them to have practical steps for leading their groups that have tangible effects and measurable success.

ELEMENTS OF A BOOT CAMP

Balancing these keys can be a challenge. You will need to provide space within the training for multiple styles of learning and interaction. Below are elements of the boot camp that we used to create these spaces.

WORSHIP

As I have stated before, the change that we need is a change of heart. We need God to give a clear vision and call leaders to his mission and work. Focusing on the practical plans and strategies will not bring life to our communities if we do not first see heart changes in our leaders. Therefore, I would strongly encourage that you set aside time for worship and prayer. This will help align your hearts toward God, and it will teach your leaders how to lead through the Spirit.

TEACHING

Each week is an opportunity to teach your leaders what you have been learning. Be sure to anchor your lessons in Scripture rather than in pragmatism. Give examples from Scripture and real life so they can put the two together. As I break down each week of the boot camp, I will summarize the teaching into two sections:

Main Point: This is the overarching theme of the week. Your goal is to have everyone understand this point before the next lesson.
Learning Objectives: This is a simple way of breaking down the main point into clear objectives for the leaders. This allows you to hone your lesson to ensure progress toward the main point while giving more specific learning goals for the leaders.

NEIGHBORHOOD INTERACTION

As I said earlier, it is important that you leave space for interaction between leaders and coaches within the relationships that they will be living out in the real world. Build your lessons to leave time for neighborhood leaders to work together to solve problems, discuss solutions, and build a plan for reaching their neighborhoods.

Discussion: For each lesson I have included discussion questions for the neighborhood groups. Use these or create your own to get leaders and coaches talking about the mission and how they can lead their people toward a bigger vision.
Neighborhood Plan: I highly recommend having leaders build a plan for reaching their neighborhoods over the course of the boot camp. This gives them consistent application of what they are learning and leaves them with a workable plan for putting these ideas into action. Reference the appendix for an example of a Neighborhood Plan.

HOMEWORK

Because this is a boot camp and you are trying to galvanize a big vision in a short period of time, homework is very beneficial. It keeps your leaders thinking about these ideas throughout the week. But most importantly, it requires your leaders to engage their neighborhoods. Discussing these ideas in a classroom is only theoretical. The homework is designed to get leaders out of their comfort zones and engaged with culture. It is also intended to build toward a comprehensive plan for missional engagement. The homework has two components:

Personal: designed to challenge the leaders to growth and dependence on God.

Group: designed to help the leaders challenge their groups and lead them to a bigger vision for their communities.

BOOT CAMP TRAJECTORY

The goal of the boot camp is to have leaders inspired by God's glory and grace, owning the mission, and leading their groups to advance the gospel in their neighborhoods. Getting leaders to that place will be a process as we deconstruct some preconceived ideas of what it means to be in and lead a community group. The following is the trajectory or progression that we used as an overlay for the training to help us achieve our goal.

Boot Camp Arch

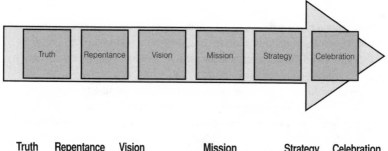

Truth	Repentance	Vision	Mission		Strategy	Celebration
Imaging God as Sender	Conviction at the Cross	Missional Realignment	Engaging Our Neighborhood	Rhythms as Lifestyle	Building with Intentionality	Putting It into Action

This trajectory helps take leaders who are at various levels of commitment to the mission of God and shepherd them through a radical change in community philosophy and purpose. It is important, however, to be flexible and to listen to where your leaders are throughout the process. You may have to slow down through some sections to help leaders get there with you. Change is hard for most people, so have compassion and patience. By providing ample time for questions and feedback, soon you will be able to celebrate with your leaders what God is doing, and is going to do, in your communities.

1. TRUTH
LESSON: "IMAGING GOD AS SENDER"

We want to start the call to change with a clear picture of God and his call on our lives. In order for leaders to change the way they think, they need to understand the arc of redemptive history. We often see our lives as a story in which God has a significant part. We want our leaders to understand that God has a big story in which we play a minor but still important role. We want them to get excited about being a part of God's mission.

The picture that Scripture gives of God is that he is sent and sending. God the Father sends Jesus, God the Son. Jesus is sent, but then sends the Holy Spirit as the Great Counselor. In this way we see the Trinity as both sent and sending. As image bearers, which we discussed in chapter 1, we are to reflect this aspect of God in our participation in the mission just as Jesus sent the disciples to be a sent and sending people. The goal at the end of this session is to challenge leaders to understand their own call as leaders and disciples of Jesus. We want them to leave with a big picture of God, his redemptive plan, and their place in it.

MAIN POINT

In the redemptive story of God, God is revealed as a sent and sending Trinity on mission. The Trinity calls us to be a people joining them on mission and living out our calling through transforming, incarnational community.

Learning Objectives
1. Students will understand that God's story frames our story, and that if the Trinity is on mission, we cannot be in God's story without being on mission with him.
2. Students will individually accept as their own the call to join God in his mission.
3. Leaders will individually accept the challenge to call their community group to partner with God in bringing the gospel to their neighborhoods.

Neighborhood Discussion

1. Discuss what it means to you personally to be called a disciple of Jesus.
2. Use the Post-it notes provided and write words or phrases describing the lives (in and out of group) of a community of disciples.
3. What are some common themes we sense as benchmarks of disciples living in community? (Facilitated exercise, and debrief of Post-its)
4. Rate your group 1, 2, 4, 5 (no 3s) on where it is on these benchmarks (1 = low).

Personal Homework

1. Read "Missional Church" by Tim Keller.[1]
2. Take a prayer walk in your neighborhood and journal your thoughts.
3. Gather calendars from all the potential "community" networks within your neighborhood (e.g., schools, social agencies, activities, rec centers, afterschool programs, organizations).
4. Write a definition of *culture*. Develop three questions that, when answered, can help you discover the culture(s) of your neighborhood.
5. Visit a potential "community" source in your neighborhood and write down some observations.

Group Homework

1. Lead a discussion in your group about the call to be disciples and what you envision your group would look like if you were spurring one another on to disciple living.
2. Help your group members see that if you are missing the missional, worship, or community component in your group, then your group does not accurately reflect the God of the Bible.
4. Lead your group in receiving God's call upon their lives and their group (being disciples on mission).

2. REPENTANCE
LESSON: "CONVICTION AT THE CROSS"

Building off session 1, this lesson intends to call leaders to a place of repentance for our apathy, fear of man, and love of life that has kept us from passionately participating in God's redemptive plan for our neighbors. Drawing from chapter 9, we want to lead to change through repentance, allowing God to change our hearts and desires before we institute a new plan or strategy. In that chapter, you will find a list of Old and New Testament examples of missional repentance that illustrates the need to repent as we move toward change.

It is also important to develop a rhythm of confession and repentance within each community group. By leading with repentance, you establish a pattern that you want leaders to follow. Additionally, Daniel 9 provides a great example of a leader confessing the sins of others. This is a great opportunity for leaders to begin to take ownership for their group and develop a communal identity.

This session should include ample time for confession, repentance, and worship. Don't just talk about it. Provide the space for frank and honest conversations about passion, devotion, and idolatry, and practice repentance. While this session will be more somber than most, it should end on the promise of God's faithfulness. Leaders should be encouraged by assurance that God is merciful and wants to see them participate in his mission.

MAIN POINT

A response to the call of God in Scripture always includes repentance. We will look at the need for repentance of sin (both omission and commission) as it relates to personal lifestyle and community group mission.

Learning Objectives

1. Learners will understand repentance as an urgent need and a rhythm to be included in personal disciplines as well as community life.
2. Each person will accept responsibility for any disobedience, idolatry, consumerism, and disregard for God's purposes.
3. Each leader will pray with neighborhood leaders to break their hearts for their neighborhoods.
4. Leaders will create a plan to lead their groups in repentance.

Neighborhood Discussion

1. What are the idols within our community groups?

2. What would it look like to dismantle these "high places"?
3. How could you call your neighborhoods and groups to repentance?
4. What would a neighborhood of repentant groups look like?

Personal Homework

1. Reflect on the centrality of the gospel and God's purpose in your own life. Where do they align and where are they disconnected? Spend some time in personal repentance.
2. Take a prayer walk looking for idols in your neighborhood. Ask God to remove them and repent of their being there.

Group Homework

1. Lead your group in discussion and repentance of idolatry.
   a. Personal
   b. Within your group
   c. In your neighborhood
2. Identify two or three lost people for each person in the group. Commit to a rhythm of praying for these people and looking for ways for them to become part of your group and experience Jesus. Make a list of the people for whom your group is praying.

3. VISION
LESSON: "MISSIONAL REALIGNMENT"

It is now time to cast a new vision for your community groups. As you have walked through repentance as leaders and with your groups, their hearts are ready for a new vision. Building from chapter 3 on ownership and chapter 5 on the neighborhood approach, the goal is to clearly define the purpose and expectation of community groups within the church.

This lesson is also when we introduce the idea of bridges and barriers from chapter 6 in preparation for the discussion on spaces and rhythms in the next two weeks. This gives group members a new category for thinking about their neighborhoods and their neighbors as they digest a new and bigger vision for community.

MAIN POINT

Vision is a combination of revelation of God and leading from God. This lesson is designed to motivate those who have repented of the distance between God's compassion for those he has created and their own. It is intended to inspire group members to step into that gap and lead communities into joining God on mission.

Learning Objectives

1. Reinforce within the minds of leaders that repentance and spiritual growth are rhythms in pursuit of intimacy with God.
2. Challenge leaders to own the mission of the church to make disciples.
3. Challenge leaders to develop their stories as gospel-telling tools to contextualize the gospel at the neighborhood and personal level.
4. Equip leaders to think through leading a group with members at various levels of spiritual maturity.

Neighborhood Discussion

1. Begin by sharing repentance experiences in neighborhood groups. Write them out.
2. What would it look like for you and your group to experience missional realignment?
3. What barriers can you identify in your neighborhood and your group?

Personal Homework

1. Prepare the story of God's initiating with you in such a way that it speaks to the barriers in your community.
2. Refine your calendar search in terms of bridges to the community in which you, your group, or your neighborhood can engage your community.

Group Homework

1. Help your group craft their individual stories to address the barriers and idols that are stumbling blocks to their friends.
2. Consider what activities you can do as a group to build bridges and dismantle barriers within your neighborhood. Write down ideas you are going to try.
3. Go on a group prayer walk, asking God to build bridges, demolish barriers, and grant your group members favor with unbelievers.

4. MISSION
LESSON: "ENGAGING OUR NEIGHBORHOOD"

With the vision set, it is time to equip leaders to own the mission in their neighborhoods. This lesson is primarily walking through chapter 6 and giving leaders a chance to discuss how their groups can live in multiple spaces. This session should include plenty of time for neighborhood discussion as well as corporate discussion. These are great opportunities to work out practical issues for living in community with a missional focus.

MAIN POINT

Mission being lived out in community is the mark of a maturing church. This lesson is designed to solidify our understanding of the importance of community groups participating in the mission of the church. This will prepare us for the following weeks as we begin to build a strategy for missional engagement within our neighborhoods.

Learning Objectives

1. Understand the dynamics of personal and group mission.
2. Begin to develop a plan that moves your group members from care focused to discipleship balanced (putting mission on the radar of what it looks like to image a sent and sending God).
3. Begin discussion of how we specifically engage our neighborhoods.

Neighborhood Discussion

1. Why would mission be a community discipline rather than an individual discipline?
2. What are the barriers for people in your groups to incorporating missional rhythms into your community?
3. How can you as a shepherd dismantle these barriers?
4. Mark down yearly events that take place in your neighborhood.
5. Mark down service and participation events that you plan to do as a neighborhood.
6. Mark down events for building community among groups in your neighborhood.

Personal Homework

1. Take the questions that you wrote in week 1 to the natural hubs of community in your neighborhood, and begin to talk to your neighbors.

Group Homework

1. Discuss what you learned about mission as a community discipline rather than an individual discipline.
2. What are the barriers for people in your group to incorporating missional rhythms into your community?
3. Mark down yearly events that take place in your neighborhood.
4. Mark down service and participation events that you plan to do as a community.

5. MISSION
LESSON: "RHYTHMS AS LIFESTYLE"

At this point it should be clear to your leaders that typical event-based community groups just aren't going to cut it. This session is about understanding how our groups can become more natural and life giving through natural rhythms rather than obligatory events. Building upon chapter 7, the goal is to show leaders how they can increase community opportunities without requiring more of their time by redeeming wasted moments. This leads to a community identity that is looking for opportunities. Again, this lesson should include plenty of time for questions and discussion on how to incorporate new rhythms into stale groups.

MAIN POINT

Sustainable community on mission has to be life giving. As leaders, you have the freedom to rethink the rhythms of your community groups. When doing so, you should consider the natural rhythms of your neighborhood and how changes would affect your ability to reach your neighbors.

Learning Objectives

1. Leaders begin to see their community groups as a lifestyle rather than an event.

2. Leaders are equipped to lead their groups to understand rhythms of community that bring life and include mission.
3. Leaders have the freedom to build life-giving rhythms into their groups.

Neighborhood Discussion
1. What are the rhythms of your community groups?
2. Make a list of life-giving rhythms and life-taking rhythms of your groups.
3. How could we redesign our groups to be more life giving?
4. Build a one-month calendar of your ideal community.

Personal Homework
1. Spend some time thinking about what your community would be like if it were life giving and more natural. What changes would you make?
2. How could you incorporate the ideas of worship, community, and mission into that group and have it remain natural and life giving?

Group Homework
1. What aspects of your group do you particularly find life giving?
2. What aspects of the group are draining?
3. What does your group have that you want to share with your nonbelieving neighbors and friends?
4. What about your group would keep you from inviting a friend/neighbor/nonbeliever?
5. Discuss an ideal rhythm of community that would be life giving to everyone.

6. STRATEGY
LESSON: "BUILDING WITH INTENTIONALITY"

This session is primarily a work party as leaders and coaches take what they have been learning and start finalizing their Neighborhood Plans. This would include a yearly calendar of events, service and participation possibilities, as well as all neighborhood hospitality functions. Stress the importance of having a plan inspired by the Holy Spirit and dependent on the Holy Spirit. If you don't have a plan, then you will not see any significant changes in the way community groups function. For this lesson, I also like to recap any areas where leaders still need clarification. By now, leaders should understand the concepts and should be focused on application.

MAIN POINT

As we move toward ownership of the mission in our community groups, it is important for us, as leaders, to begin to think strategically about our neighborhood. We have been called to make disciples, so how and when are we going to provide the opportunities for that to happen? This week we will continue to develop our plan for reaching our neighborhood and discuss the opportunities we have as a neighborhood of groups to engage the culture around us.

Learning Objectives

1. Address questions and complete the Group Plan; build a community that is on mission.
2. Understand the role of other groups in your neighborhood when it comes to mission.
3. Build a calendar for your group that gets you thinking strategically about how your group engages with your neighborhood.

Neighborhood Discussion

1. Complete the Neighborhood Plan.
2. Discuss a rhythm of connection as leaders to ensure the plan gets carried out.

Personal Homework

1. Review the Neighborhood Plan and write down thoughts in preparation for next week's boot camp discussion.

Group Homework

1. Work with your community group to finish the Group Plan.

7. CELEBRATION
"PUTTING IT INTO ACTION"

The last week of the boot camp should be one of celebration. This is a time to let each neighborhood group share what God has taught them throughout the boot camp. This provides an opportunity for other leaders to be inspired and challenged by the innovation they see happening in other groups. It also provides encouragement as each leader gets a glimpse of how each group participating in the mission of God can make a huge difference to the kingdom. By announcing the goals of each group and neighborhood for replication and conversions, you begin to see how God wants to impact your city.

11

HISTORY

THE MARS HILL STORY

At this point we have covered quite a bit of ground. We started with laying a biblical foundation for the importance of community within the Christian life and the church. From there, we explored the need for every member to own the mission of your church and build a strategy for reaching your city from that premise. Finally, we talked about how we inspire change within a ministry that has become used to having a machine do all the breathing.

Although it may be daunting if you are in that situation, I want to assure you that change is possible. As Paul said, God is "making his appeal through us."[1] God's picture of community can be found in Acts 2, 1 Peter 2, Ephesians 4, and Colossians 3. If this is the inspired picture of his community, then it must be possible through dependence on Jesus and the help of the Holy Spirit.

To assure you that change is possible, I want to tell you the story of the evolution of community at Mars Hill Church. Mars Hill has experienced an enormous amount of blessing and grace from God over its fourteen years of existence. As I talk with pastors around the country, though, I fear there is a perception that we have it all figured out.

To let you behind the curtain a bit, it should be noted that we have leaned on that grace a lot over the years. Ministry at Mars Hill is often described as holding on to a kite in a hurricane. As the Spirit moves, we are often tossed about and straining to keep up. Community at Mars Hill has been no exception.

We have had to make many adjustments to keep up with the growth and changes in the church. My hope is that by hearing a bit of our story, you will be encouraged by the amount of change that can occur, even in a large organization, and be inspired to not fear mistakes.

Let me be clear that this is not the way I would encourage you to let community groups evolve at your church. This is descriptive of our journey, not prescriptive. My hope is that you will have a long-term vision from the start and build community on that trajectory from the beginning. With that said, let's take a look at the evolution of community groups at Mars Hill.

PHASE ONE: THE TIME OF THE JUDGES

ATTENDANCE: 30–200

LEADER AS TEACHER

Deuteronomy 12:8 describes the time of the judges as a time when "everyone [was] doing whatever [was] right in his own eyes." This is an appropriate description of community in the early stages of Mars Hill. Mars Hill began as a community group in Pastor Mark Driscoll's home. It wasn't called a community group then—it was the whole church—but it consisted of around thirty people who would gather in Driscoll's living room to study Scripture.

As the church grew from that original core, community was left to develop naturally. When the church was less than a hundred people, this worked fine, as everyone more or less felt connected. But as the church grew, this started to show as a deficiency within the church, even though "community" was one of four stated values. Growth was happening so fast that we didn't have time for our theology of community to keep up. In an effort to address this deficiency, elders and some key leaders began to lead their own Bible studies, and random groups popped up wherever people thought it was a good idea in their own eyes.

The decision to go with Bible studies stemmed from a real need within the church. Because we were situated in the least churched city in America, very few of the first-generation Mars Hillians had good doctrine. The few that were "churched" came from churches that did not hold a high view of Scripture.

While these groups did address the need for increasing the biblical IQ of the church, they had their drawbacks. Most leaders' only example of a Bible teacher was Mark, who is an extremely literate and intelligent teacher. This resulted in groups led by people trying to be mini-Marks, with stacks of commentaries and Hebrew lexicons. The groups resembled classrooms more than they did communities, and leaders used groups as an audience for their preaching.

These groups were theologically robust but they were not the most welcoming. Additionally, such groups created a culture that made it feel as though you needed a PhD to lead a group, which stunted the growth of groups. Still, this did not stem the tide of growth with which God was blessing the church.

PHASE 2: RESPONDING TO GROWTH

ATTENDANCE: 200–500

LEADER AS FACILITATOR

As the gap grew wider between attendance and people in community, we recognized the limitations of the current manifestation of community groups and the impact on developing leaders. In response, community groups were overhauled, and a new vision was cast to recruit more leaders. Because we needed to make up ground quickly, and in response to the stunting effect of a high bar of leadership, we asked leaders to simply be facilitators of a community group. The responsibility of leaders would be to keep the conversation moving and encourage the participation of every person. The last regime had seen leaders as teachers. This new manifestation saw leaders as facilitators.

This structure got rid of the classroom atmosphere and opened the door for more leaders. It provided a boost for group growth, but we did not have a good mechanism for oversight. All group leaders reported to one director. Leaders were required to go to a training class and were left primarily on their own after that.

As attendance continued to increase by over 60 percent annually, organization was becoming a problem. Additionally, while group growth had been addressed by making leaders facilitators, groups did little to develop actual community. Community groups continued to feel like an additional event rather than a community.

PHASE 3: THE AGE OF THE SHEPHERD

ATTENDANCE: 500–2,000

LEADER AS SHEPHERD

Up to this point, oversight of community groups was one job among several for which an elder who drew the short straw had to take responsibility. It was not that we did not see the importance of community groups, but it was difficult to give them the attention they needed among other daily responsibilities. It was at this time that we realized the trouble we would be in if we did not develop a scalable community group strategy before growth got out of hand.

As Mars Hill was now growing into the thousands, we realized we needed a plan to provide pastoral care for the church, or to punt it like so many other large churches had done. Our convictions would not let us punt, so we began to build the plan that has evolved into today's community group structure.

The first thing we did was redefine the leader role. A facilitator of a discussion would never address the need for real community or pastoral care. So we called our leaders to be shepherds, caring for the ten to twelve people in their groups. This was a significant paradigm shift for our leaders, but it began the transition to groups that felt like a family rather than a book club.

Next, we instituted the coaching structure to care for the leaders as well as the members. It took several iterations of span-of-care and expectations to get coaching right, but this changed the leadership and pastoral care structure of the church for the better. We were on the right track and now had a scalable structure for growth. It was also during this phase that we began to organize groups by regions of the city. We only had one campus, but we had groups strewn about the Puget Sound. This structure helped us to better care for leaders and to build a framework for the future campus expansion.

PHASE 4: COMMUNITY ON MISSION
ATTENDANCE 2,000–10,000+

LEADER AS DISCIPLE MAKER

This brings us up to the present phase of community at Mars Hill. As the church went multisite, the groups were already organized in such a way as to facilitate a shift. Coaches and head coaches for regions became the community group leaders at the various campuses.

It was at this time that we realized that we were missing an opportunity to affect our city and we were not developing mature disciples. While we had been successful in building real community, few of our members were actually participating in the mission of God. We needed our shepherds to be shepherding their people to mission as well as worship of God and love for one another. We needed our leaders to be disciple makers.

This realization was the impetus for the first boot camp that was outlined in chapter 10. While we are still working on becoming a church of disciples and disciple makers on mission, we feel that we finally have a structure, strategy, and philosophy that will help us to make an eternal impact on our city.

One key to understanding the growth of community groups at Mars Hill is seeing how God added layers to our community to develop mature disciples. We did not run in one direction and then stop and run in another. Rather, God added each as a layer upon the previous layer, which allowed us to have a foundation of biblical knowledge and dependence. A true understanding of the revelation of Scripture should lead to love for God and one another. And as we've discussed, that love is intended to manifest in the mission of God.

Evolution of Community Group Expectations

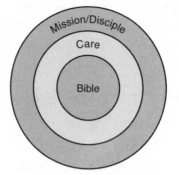

As we put these layers together within community, we are able to disciple the church toward an identity in Christ that expresses itself in worship to God, love for one another, and compassion for the lost. If I were you, I would jump to this last phase and let our mistakes be your lesson. While our experience shows that you can change the culture of a large church, even four times, it would be much easier to get it right the first time.

THEREFORE, GO AND MAKE DISCIPLES

Your community groups can become a source of life not only for the people of your church, but also they can become a beacon of life for the people of your city. Within your community groups are God's chosen heralds of the gospel. God has determined that he would make his appeal for salvation through his people. This is an invaluable resource to steward.

Don't be content with less than the community of God in lock step with the redemptive plan of God. As I said in the introduction, the world will never recover from such a community of God's people living lives to glorify Jesus. As we lift up Jesus in our community groups, we will experience the life-giving, soul-sustaining joy that comes from aligning our hearts with the purposes of God.

In this way our community groups will not only be brought back to life, but they also will beget life. This is the promise of God and our joy. May Jesus get the glory for every breath taken.

GROUP PLAN

INFORMATION
Neighborhood:

Coach:

Leader:

Missiologist:

Administrator:

Host:

Social Coordinator:

GOALS AND PROJECTIONS
Culture or people group focus:

Number of people that our group is praying will come to Christ this year through the group:

Names of people that our group is praying would come to know Christ this year through the group:

Number of groups we want to see replicated this year to reach more people in our neighborhoods:

OPPORTUNITIES

Participation:

Building Relationships:

Service:

Loving the City:

Hospitality:

Invitation into Community:

Gospel Community:

Transformation through prayer, Bible study, confession, repentance, etc.:

Does our group have an understanding of how natural rhythms (activities we participate in anyway) can become an important part of a missional community group?

NEIGHBORHOOD PLAN

INFORMATION
Neighborhood:

Coach:

Number of Groups in Our Neighborhood:

RESOURCES
Locations of Natural Community:

Service and Event Agencies:

Local Papers and Newsletters:

GOALS
Vision for Our Neighborhood:

How many people are we praying to see come to Christ through community groups in the next year?

Number of groups currently in our neighborhood:

Projected number of groups in:
- 3 months:
- 6 months:
- 12 months:

How many apprentices or new leaders do we need in the next year?

COMMUNITY GROUP REPLICATION PLAN

INFORMATION

Community Group Coach:

Community Group Leader:

Apprentice:

Neighborhood:

REPLICATION GOALS

1. Advance the gospel of Jesus Christ and plant more communities.
2. Produce more opportunities for people to see and experience the gospel.
3. Continue to create compassion for those who don't know Jesus or don't have community.
4. Grow as disciples and make disciples.

REPLICATION VISION

How many people do we pray for?

When do we want to replicate to achieve the above goals?

Who or what is our mission field?

Who are our potential apprentices?

Where are our potential host sites?

STEPS FOR REPLICATION READINESS

1. Identify Apprentice
2. Vision for Group
3. Core Group
4. Host Location (mission before opportunity)
5. Replication Timeline

This next section should include dates when the apprentice leads the group, a replication party, and a launch date.

Date:

Event:

Location:

JOB DESCRIPTION: COMMUNITY GROUP LEADER

ORIENTATION
Toward members and group

QUALIFICATIONS
Mature and growing disciple of Jesus and well grounded in Scripture

Member of the church

Committed to the purpose and values of the church

Genuine love for people along with demonstrated relational skills

Ability to both challenge and encourage others in their walks with the Lord

Humble demeanor and teachable spirit; consistent and reliable

Good verbal skills and possesses the ability to communicate with warmth and graciousness in such a way that is clear and understandable

Solid reputation (above reproach) inside and outside the church, meeting the requirements of 1 Timothy 3

Willing to be judged with greater strictness as a leader in the church (James 3:1)

Ability to lead 8–16 people

Additionally, leading a community group is a deacon role at Mars Hill Church, and therefore the qualifications of a deacon from Acts 6:1–7 and 1 Timothy 3:8–13 apply:

Worthy of respect

Sincere

Not indulging in much wine (self-controlled and without addictions)

Not pursuing dishonest gain

Keeping hold of the truths of faith with a clear conscience

Tested and affirmed

RESPONSIBILITIES

Shepherd: Care for and lead your community group toward growth as disciples of Jesus. Although you are not required to be the agent of the following for every member of your group, you should take responsibility to make sure each item is occurring:

Discipleship: Know the members of your group and encourage growth through the use of a discipleship plan.

Call on others in your group to shepherd one another and provide an atmosphere that is challenging and full of grace.

Facilitate fellowship times with Scripture (sermon-based), prayer, worship, confession, and repentance.

Designate members of your group for 1:1 discipleship with new or nonbelievers.

Membership: Encourage people to become committed members of the church and address lapsed expectations of members, such as community involvement, service, and giving.

Missiologist: Lead your group in the mission of the church.

Create a Group Plan in conjunction with the Neighborhood Plan.

Cast vision and pursue opportunities for neighborhood involvement.

Network with other groups in your neighborhood.

Grow your group through missional efforts and seek to replicate to advance gospel opportunities in your neighborhood.

Develop future leaders by apprenticing members of your group.

Administrator: Organize and plan so that your group functions well.

Maintain group information and contact list.

Maintain clear communication to the group.

Provide clear expectations and safe places to gather.

Note: While a community group leader is responsible for all three areas above, the leader does not need to fill every one of these roles. Generally the leader will be the shepherd of the group but does not necessarily have to be its chief missiologist or administrator. These roles can be delegated to members of the group based on spiritual gifts and passions.

JOB DESCRIPTION: COMMUNITY GROUP COACH

ORIENTATION
Toward leaders and neighborhood

QUALIFICATIONS
Mature and growing disciple of Jesus, and well grounded in Scripture

Member of the church

Committed to the purpose and values of the church

Genuine love for people along with demonstrated relational skills

Ability to both challenge and encourage others in their walks with the Lord

Humble demeanor and teachable spirit; consistent and reliable

Good verbal skills and possesses the ability to communicate with warmth and graciousness in such a way that is clear and understandable

Willing to be judged with greater strictness as a leader in the church (James 3:1)

Ability to lead 40–60 people

Additionally, coaching may be seen as a deacon role within the church, and therefore the qualifications of a deacon from Acts 6:1–7 and 1 Timothy 3:8–13 apply:

Worthy of respect

Sincere

Not indulging in much wine (self-controlled and without addictions)

Not pursuing dishonest gain

Keeping hold of the truths of faith with a clear conscience

Tested and affirmed

RESPONSIBILITIES

Shepherd: Care for the leaders in your huddle.

    Shepherd leaders in areas of spiritual, familial, vocational, and physical health.

    Coach leaders in their shepherding of their groups.

    Address appropriate levels of care and discipline within groups in your care.

Missiologist: Coach your leaders to engage in the mission.

    Own the mission, replication, and leadership development for your groups.

    Coach leaders in opportunities to engage in the neighborhood.

    Participate in prayer for your neighborhood.

    Challenge and help leaders think through alternative rhythms.

    Mobilize groups for cooperative hospitality, service, and participation events.

    Work with your head coach to develop a Neighborhood Plan.

Administrator: Organize and plan so that your groups function well together in your neighborhood.

    Ensure each group has a Group Plan that is aligned with the Neighborhood Plan.

    Track and ensure apprentice leadership in each of your groups.

    Help develop, review, and approve Replication Plans for each of your groups.

JOB DESCRIPTION: HEAD COACH/ COMMUNITY PASTOR

Note: Churches/campuses may not have a head coaching role until group density dictates. Context and density will dictate the scope of this role. Urban campuses will have head coaches/ community pastors over neighborhoods, while rural campuses may have them leading cities or regions.

ORIENTATION
Toward coaches and neighborhood

QUALIFICATIONS
Mature and growing disciple of Jesus and well grounded in Scripture

Member of the church

Committed to the purpose and values of the church

Genuine love for people along with demonstrated relational skills

Ability to both challenge and encourage others in their walks with the Lord

Humble demeanor and teachable spirit; consistent and reliable

Good verbal skills and possesses the ability to communicate with warmth and graciousness in such a way that is clear and understandable

Willing to be judged with greater strictness as a leader in the church (James 3:1)

Ability to lead 100–250 people

Additionally, head coaching may be considered a deacon role, and therefore the qualifications of a deacon from Acts 6:1–7 and 1 Timothy 3:8–13 apply (qualifications for an elder/pastor can be found in 1 Timothy 3:1–7 and Titus 1:6–9):

Worthy of respect

Sincere

Not indulging in much wine (self-controlled and without
addictions)

Not pursuing dishonest gain

Keeping hold of the truths of faith with a clear conscience

Tested and affirmed

RESPONSIBILITIES

Shepherd: Care for the coaches in your neighborhood.

Shepherd coaches in areas of spiritual, familial, vocational, and
physical health.

Help coaches in their shepherding of their leaders.

Address appropriate levels of care and discipline within groups in
your neighborhood.

Missiologist: Lead the mission in your neighborhood.

Develop a Neighborhood Plan with the help of your coaches and
leaders.

Lead your neighborhood in prayer for the advancement of the
gospel.

Own the mission, replication, and leadership development for
your neighborhood.

Ensure mission ownership throughout your neighborhood.

Mobilize groups for cooperative hospitality, service, and participation events.

Administrator: Organize and plan at the neighborhood level to ensure
progress toward stated goals.

Ensure progress toward goals set in your Neighborhood Plan.

Track and ensure apprentice leadership and Replication Plans in
your neighborhood.

NOTES

DIAGNOSIS: AN INTRODUCTION
1. 1 Cor. 1:2–4.
2. 1 Cor. 15:58.
3. John 10:10.
4. See John Piper, *Don't Waste Your Life* (Wheaton, IL: Crossway, 2003), 107–30, and "Romans: The Greatest Letter Ever Written," John Piper, accessed in June 2010, http://www.desiringgod.org/resource-library/series-index/romans-the-greatest-letter-ever-written.
5. 1 Pet. 5:8.
6. 1 Pet. 2:11.
7. 1 Tim. 6:12; 1 Cor. 16:13.
8. Mark Driscoll and Gerry Breshears, *Vintage Church: Timeless Truths and Timely Methods* (Wheaton, IL: Crossway, 2008), 38.
9. Matt. 28:19–20.
10. 1 Pet. 2:9.
11. 1 Pet. 2:9–12.
12. Bill Clem, "It's All About Jesus: Community," accessed in September 2009, http://www.marshillchurch.org/media/its-all-about-jesus/its-all-about-jesus-community.

PART ONE
THE FOUNDATION: BUILDING BLOCKS FOR LIFE
1. Matt. 7:24–27.

CHAPTER 1: IMAGE
1. While the ontological nature of the Trinity was not broken on the cross, Jesus did experience the relational separation from the Father as he received the Father's wrath for our sin. Matt. 27:46; Wayne A. Grudem, *Systematic Theology: An Introduction to Biblical Doctrine* (Grand Rapids, MI: Zondervan, 2009), 574; Justin S. Holcomb and Lindsey A. Holcomb, *Rid of My Disgrace: Hope and Healing for Victims of Sexual Assault* (Wheaton, IL: Crossway, 2011), 112.
2. Gen. 3:8.
3. Dietrich Bonhoeffer, *Life Together*, trans. John W. Doberstein (New York: Harper & Row, 1954), 24.
4. Eph. 2:7.
5. Gen. 1:26. For an examination of the plural language used here, see John H. Sailhamer, *The Pentateuch as Narrative: A Biblical-Theological Commentary* (Grand Rapids, MI: Zondervan, 1992), 95–96.
6. For more on being created in the image of God, see Anthony A. Hoekema, *Created in God's Image* (Grand Rapids, MI: Eerdmans, 1986).
7. Gen. 2:18. Also see Sailhamer, *The Pentateuch as Narrative*, 101–102.
8. Westminster Assembly, *The Shorter Catechism* (1647), accessed in July 2010, http://www.creeds.net/Westminster/shorter_catechism.html.
9. Ex. 34:6–7.
10. Col. 3:12–17.
11. Isaiah 6.
12. Mark 14:69–71.
13. Eusebius, *Church History* 3.1.2.
14. John 1:14–16.
15. 2 Tim. 2:8–10.
16. John 14:26.
17. 2 Pet. 1:3 (NIV).
18. Eph. 2:19–22, cf. 1 Pet. 2:5.
19. 1 Pet. 2:9.

20. 1 Pet. 2:9.

21. 1 Pet. 2:9.

22. 1 Pet. 2:10.

23. 1 Pet. 2:11–12.

24. Bonhoeffer, *Life Together*, 23.

25. 1 Pet. 2:11.

26. 1 Pet. 2:12.

27. 1 Pet. 2:12.

28. John 13:34–35.

29. John Piper, *Desiring God* (Sisters, OR: Multnomah, 2003), 50.

30. 1 Pet. 2:12.

31. Christopher J. H. Wright, *The Mission of God: Unlocking the Bible's Grand Narrative* (Downers Grove, IL: InterVarsity, 2006), 333.

32. Mark Driscoll, personal conversation with the author about the theology of community, January 20, 2010.

33. John 1:14.

34. 2 Pet. 1:3.

35. 1 Pet. 2:9–10.

CHAPTER 2: BODY

1. Sinclair B. Ferguson, *Grow in Grace* (Edinburgh: Banner of Truth, 1989), 67.

2. The National Study of Youth and Religion (NSYR) is the most comprehensive and rigorous social scientific research ever conducted on the religious and spiritual lives of American youth. The wave one survey was conducted among American youth ages thirteen to seventeen between July 2002 and April 2003, and produced a total N = 3370. Most recently, a third wave of the survey was conducted from September 24, 2007, through April 21, 2008, with the same respondents—when they were between the ages of eighteen and twenty-three. The NSYR is under the direction of Christian Smith of the Department of Sociology at the University of Notre Dame. For methodological details and related publications, visit: http://www.youthandreligion.org/. The findings reported here were calculated using publicly available data, accessible online here: http://www.thearda.com/Archive/Files/Descriptions/NSYRW3.asp. Data were weighted appropriately.

3. This is one-third (33.5 percent) of the national sample of adults ages eighteen to twenty-three.

4. Again, this includes those who simply attend an evangelical church every so often but may not self-identify as evangelical Christians. Of course, many of them do. This also includes emerging adults ages eighteen to twenty-three who identity as evangelical Christians but who are not involved in any church.

5. Matt. 28:18–20.

6. Matt. 25:23.

7. James 1:22.

8. James 2:17.

9. Rom. 7:23; 2 Cor. 10:1–4; 1 Tim. 1:18; James 4:1; 1 Pet. 2:11.

10. Timothy S. Lane and Paul David Tripp, *How People Change* (Greensboro, NC: New Growth, 2006), 73–90.

11. For more on the importance of preaching, see Driscoll and Breshears, *Vintage Church*, 85–109.

12. Heb. 13:17.

13. Exodus 18.

14. Acts 6:1–6; Titus 1:5.

15. For more information about Redemption Groups, see Mike Wilkerson, *Redemption: Freed by Jesus from the Idols We Worship and the Wounds We Carry* (Wheaton, IL: Crossway, 2011).

16. John 13:14, 34–35; Rom. 1:12; 12:10, 16; 13:8; 14:13; 15:7, 14; 16:16; 1 Cor. 1:10; 11:33; 12:25; Gal. 5:13, 15, 26; 6:2; Eph. 4:2, 16, 32; 5:19, 21; Phil. 2:3–5; 4:2; Col. 3:9, 13, 16; 1 Thess. 3:12; 4:9, 18; 5:11, 13, 15; 2 Thess. 1:3; Heb. 3:13; 10:24–25; 13:1; James 4:11; 5:9, 16; 1 Pet. 3:8; 4:8–9; 5:5; 1 John 1:7; 3:11, 23; 4:7, 11–12.

17. Ed Stetzer, "The Church Defined: Gospel Community in Context" (lecture, Advance10 Conference, Advance the Church: Contextualizing the Gospel in the New South,

Raleigh-Durham, NC, April 2010, accessed in August 2010, http://advancethechurch
.com/2010/05/05/advance10-conference-speaker-audio-and-worship-set-list/).

18. Ed Stetzer, "Missional Missiology" (series of lectures for Re:Train, Mars Hill Church, Seattle, WA, November 13–14, 2009).

19. Stetzer, "Missional Missiology."

20. Rom. 16:26.

21. 1 Cor. 3:1–2; Heb. 5:12–13.

22. 1 Cor. 3:6–9.

23. Acts 2:41–47.

24. James 1:22.

CHAPTER 3: OWNERSHIP

1. 2 Cor. 5:20.

2. Alan Hirsch, "Session 1," (lecture, Acts 29 Midwest Quarterly 3, August 17, 2010, http://www.acts29network.org/sermon/acts-29-midwest-quarterly—session-1-alan -hirsch/).

3. Rom. 15:6.

4. Matt. 28:18–20.

5. Stetzer, "Missional Missiology."

6. 1 Thess. 3:2.

7. Hirsch, "Session 1."

8. Lesslie Newbigin, *The Open Secret: An Introduction to the Theology of Mission* (Grand Rapids, MI: Eerdmans, 1995), 1.

9. 1 Pet. 2:9–12.

10. 1 John 4:19.

11. Matt. 5:31–46.

12. James 2:17, 26.

13. James 1:22.

14. James 1:27.

15. Luke 9:60.

16. Eph. 1:13–14.

17. Hirsch, "Session 1."

18. "Who Do You Play For?" *Miracle*, directed by Gavin O'Connor (Burbank, CA: Walt Disney Studios Home Entertainment, 2004) DVD.

19. Isa. 6:1–8.

20. Acts 1:1–11.

21. Acts 22.

22. 1 Pet. 2:9–12.

23. 1 Pet. 2:12.

24. Hirsch, "Session 1."

25. 1 Cor. 12:21–25.

26. This idea is adapted from Ori Brafman and Rod A. Beckstrom, *The Starfish and the Spider: The Unstoppable Power of Leaderless Organizations* (New York: Penguin Group, 2006).

27. Hirsch, "Session 1."

28. Matt. 28:20.

29. Ps. 51:12–13.

30. Hirsch, "Session 1."

PART TWO
HEALTH PLAN: REDEFINING COMMUNITY GROUPS

1. Col. 3:12–17.

2. John Piper, "Let the Nations Be Glad," parts 1 and 2 (lecture, Advance09 Resurgence Conference, Raleigh-Durham, NC, June 4–6, 2009, http://theresurgence.com/advance _conference_2009.)

CHAPTER 4: COMMUNITY

1. Matt. 7:16–20; 12:33; Luke 6:43–44.

2. C. S. Lewis, *The Weight of Glory* (New York: HarperCollins, 2001), 26.

3. Rom. 1:25.

4. Bill Clem, *Disciple* (Wheaton, IL: Crossway, 2011).

5. Gen. 1:27–28; Eph. 2:8–10.

6. Rom. 5:10.

7. 2 Cor. 5:18.

8. Rom. 3:25.

9. Isa. 61:10.

10. Rom. 8:23.

11. 1 Cor. 6:20.

12. See Ps. 30:4; 59:16; 100; 150; John 4:23–24; Rom. 12:1; 1 Tim. 2:8; Heb. 12:28–29; 1 Pet. 2:5. For further reading, see Harold M. Best, *Unceasing Worship: Biblical Perspectives on Worship and the Arts* (Downers Grove, IL: InterVarsity, 2003).

13. 1 Pet. 2:9.

14. Gen. 1:26–27.

15. John 1:1–5, 14.

16. Gen. 1:26.

17. Heb. 10:24–26; 2 Cor. 5:18.

18. John 1:14.

19. 1 Pet. 2:12.

20. Matt. 28:19; Luke 10:27; Jer. 29:5.

21. 2 Pet. 3:9.

22. 1 Pet. 2:9–12.

23. 1 Pet. 2:9, cf. 1 Pet. 1:2.

24. 1 Pet. 2:9, cf. 1 Tim. 2:5.

25. 1 Pet. 2:9, cf. Rom. 4:5–8.

26. Rom. 6:18.

27. 1 Pet. 2:9.

28. 1 Pet. 2:10.

29. See John Piper, *Don't Waste Your Life* (Wheaton, IL: Crossway, 2003), 107–130.

30. 1 Pet. 2:12.

31. Wilkerson, *Redemption* and Tim Chester, *You Can Change: God's Transforming Power for Our Sinful Behavior and Negative Emotions* (Wheaton, IL: Crossway, 2010) are great resources for equipping your groups with the truths of the gospel.

32. John Piper, "How Important Is Church Membership?" (lecture, Bethlehem Baptist Church and Desiring God, July 13, 2008), http://www.desiringgod.org/ResourceLibrary/Sermons/ByDate/2008/2989_How_Important_Is_Church_Membership/.

33. Acts 2:42.

34. Acts 2:42.

35. 1 Cor. 15:35–58.

36. For further reading, see John Owen, *The Mortification of Sin in Believers* (London: The Religious Tract Society, 1842).

37. 1 Pet. 2:9.

38. For further reading, see Wilkerson, *Redemption*.

39. Acts 2:42.

40. Acts 2:44–46.

41. 2 Cor. 5:20.

42. Acts 2:43.

43. Acts 2:47.

CHAPTER 5: NEIGHBORHOOD

1. 1 Cor. 9:20–22.

2. Peter Block, *Community: The Structure of Belonging* (San Francisco: Berrett-Koehler, 2008), 1–2.

3. 1 Pet. 2:10.

4. Robert D. Putnam, *Bowling Alone: The Collapse and Revival of Amercian Community* (New York: Simon and Schuster, 2000), 71–72. Putnam summarizes statistics from the 1952 National Election Study, which found 23 percent membership in religious groups, excluding church membership; a 1955 survey, reported by Hausknecht, *The Joiners* (25 percent); the 1987 General Social Survey (14 percent); a 1989 survey, reported by

Verba, Schlozman, and Brady, *Voice and Equality* (8 percent); and the 1996 National Election Study (13 percent).

5. Putnam, *Bowling Alone*, 72.

6. Putnam, *Bowling Alone*, 72.

7. Block, *Community*, 1.

8. Block, *Community*, 93.

9. Matt. 4:18–19; Mark 1:16–17.

10. Ed Stetzer and David Putnam, *Breaking the Missional Code: Your Church Can Become a Missionary in Your Community* (Nashville, TN: Broadman and Holman, 2006).

11. John 17.

12. For example, see "American Congregations at the Beginning of the Twenty-First Century," National Congregations Study, accessed in June 2010, http://www.soc.duke.edu/natcong/Docs/NCSII_report_final.pdf.

13. Exodus 18.

CHAPTER 6: SPACES

1. Daniel Sanchez, "Biblical Storying" (class lecture notes, Southwestern Baptist Theological Seminary, Fort Worth, TX, January 2005).

2. 1 Cor. 9:22.

3. Mark Driscoll has been using this taxonomy at Mars Hill for years. For example, see Mark Driscoll, "Redeeming Greatness: Luke 9:46–50" (sermon, Mars Hill Church, Seattle, WA, August 15, 2010), http://www.marshillchurch.org/media/luke/redeeming-greatness. Also see Mark Driscoll, *The Radical Reformission: Reaching Out without Selling Out* (Grand Rapids, MI: Zondervan, 2004).

4. Block, *Community*, 43.

5. Joseph R. Myers, *The Search to Belong: Rethinking Intimacy, Community, and Small Groups* (Grand Rapids, MI: Zondervan, 2003).

6. Edward T. Hall, *The Hidden Dimension* (New York: Anchor, 1990).

7. Block, *Community*, 29.

8. Driscoll, *The Radical Reformission*, 139–57.

9. 1 Pet. 2:12; cf. Matt. 5:16.

10. Jer. 29:4–7.

11. Matt. 28:19–20.

12. 1 Pet. 2:12.

CHAPTER 7: RHYTHMS

1. Luke 5:37.

2. Brad J. Waggoner, *The Shape of Faith to Come: Spiritual Formation and the Future of Discipleship* (Nashville, TN: Broadman and Holman, 2008), 170.

3. Emily Anthes, "Building around the Mind," *Scientific American Mind* (April–June 2009), 53.

4. Bill Bright, *The Four Spiritual Laws* (Orlando, FL: New Life, 1968), accessed in May 2010, http://campuscrusade.com/fourlawseng.htm. This evangelistic Christian tract was written by Bill Bright, founder of Campus Crusade for Christ, as a means to clearly explain the essentials of the Christian faith concerning salvation.

5. Rom. 12:15.

6. For an in-depth explanation and application of the theology of *Christus Victor*, see "Demons Are Tormenting Me: Jesus Is Katie's *Christus Victor*," in *Death by Love: Letters from the Cross* by Mark Driscoll and Gerry Breshears (Wheaton, IL: Crossway, 2008), 37–55.

7. Tim Chester and Steve Timmis, *Total Church: A Radical Reshaping around Gospel and Community* (Wheaton, IL: Crossway, 2008), 63

8. Magali Rheault, "Eating Out: For the Love of Food," *Kiplinger's Personal Finance*, October 2000, 30.

CHAPTER 8: STRUCTURE

1. Chester and Timmis, *Total Church*.

2. Num. 12:3 (NIV).

3. Clem, *Disciple*.

4. Larry Osborne, *Sticky Church* (Grand Rapids, MI: Zondervan, 2008).

5. For more on this subject, see Carson Pue, *Mentoring Leaders: Developing Character, Calling, and Competency* (Grand Rapids, MI: Baker, 2005).

6. See Bill Hybels, *Courageous Leadership* (Grand Rapids, MI: Zondervan, 2002), 44.

PART THREE
TREATMENT: EFFECTING CHANGE IN YOUR GROUPS

1. George Carlin, *Brain Droppings* (New York: Hyperion, 1997), 197.

CHAPTER 9: REPENTANCE

1. 2 Cor. 6:1–2.

2. 2 Cor. 5:17–6:2.

3. 2 Tim. 2:10.

4. 1 Cor. 9:22.

5. George Whitefield, *Selected Sermons of George Whitefield*, ed. A. R. Buckland (Philadelphia, PA: The Union, 1904), 64.

6. 2 Chron. 34:27.

7. Gal. 5:16.

8. Richard Baxter, *The Reformed Pastor*, ed. William Brown (Whitefish, MT: Kessinger, 2006), 73.

9. Rev. 2:2–5.

10. Matt. 10:34–39.

11. 1 Tim. 1:18.

12. 2 Cor. 6:1–7.

13. Numbers 14.

14. Owen, *The Mortification of Sin*, 9.

15. 1 Pet. 5:8.

16. Mark 4:15.

17. 2 Cor. 2:11; Eph. 4:27.

18. Charles H. Spurgeon, "The Ethiopian" (sermon no. 2536), in *The Metropolitan Tabernacle Pulpit*, vol. 43 (London: Pilgrim, 1897), 462. Also see http://www.spurgeongems.org/vols43-45/chs2536.pdf, page 4.

19. John 14:6.

20. 2 Thess. 1:8–9.

21. John 12:25.

22. Eph. 6:12; Matt. 9:37–38.

23. Matt 9:37; John 4:35.

24. 1 Tim. 1:15.

25. Matt. 10:28.

26. Prov. 9:10.

27. 2 Tim. 1:6–7.

28. Rom. 6:11.

29. Rom. 5:8, 10.

30. 2 Pet. 1:3.

31. John 14:16, 26.

32. 2 Cor. 5:17; Romans 6.

33. 2 Cor. 6:2.

34. Piper, *Don't Waste Your Life*, 110.

CHAPTER 10: BOOT CAMP

1. Tim Keller, "Missional Church" (sermon, June 2001), http://download.redeemer.com/pdf/learn/resources/Missional_Church-Keller.pdf.

CHAPTER 11: HISTORY

1. 2 Cor. 5:20.

GENERAL INDEX

SCRIPTURE INDEX

 # RE:LIT

Resurgence Literature (Re:Lit) is a ministry of the Resurgence. At www.theResurgence.com you will find free theological resources in blog, audio, video, and print forms, along with information on forthcoming conferences, to help Christians contend for and contextualize Jesus's gospel. At www.ReLit.org you will also find the full lineup of Resurgence books for sale. The elders of Mars Hill Church have generously agreed to support Resurgence and the Acts 29 Church Planting Network in an effort to serve the entire church.

FOR MORE RESOURCES

Re:Lit – www.relit.org
Resurgence – www.theResurgence.com
Re:Train – www.retrain.org
Mars Hill Church – www.marshillchurch.org
Acts 29 – www.acts29network.org